D1309860

Perl™!

I Didn't Know You Could Do That...™

Martin C. Brown

SYBEX®

San Francisco • Paris • Düsseldorf • Soest • London

Associate Publisher: Richard Mills
Contracts and Licensing Manager: Kristine O'Callaghan
Acquisitions and Developmental Editor: Diane Lowery
Editor: Joseph A. Webb
Production Editor: Liz Burke
Technical Editor: David Medinets
Book Designers: Franz Baumhackl, Kate Kaminski
Electronic Publishing Specialists: Jill Niles,
    Maureen Forys, Sharon Page Ritchie
Proofreader: Laurie O'Connell
Indexer: Ann Rogers
CD Coordinator: Kara Eve Schwartz
CD Technicians: Keith McNeil, Siobhan Dowling
Cover Designer: Daniel Ziegler
Cover Illustrator/Photographer: PhotoDisc

Library of Congress Card Number: 00-107728

ISBN: 0-7821-2862-9

Manufactured in the United States of America

10 9 8 7 6 5 4 3 2 1

Acknowledgments

First and foremost, I need to thank those people at Sybex who helped me to produce the book and stuck with me when it didn't go according to plan. The list includes, but is not exclusive to, Diane Lowery, Denise Santoro Lincoln, Liz Burke, Rodda League, Jill Niles, Maureen Forys, Sharon Page Ritchie, and Dan Mummert.

I also need to thank Joe Webb, who copyedited the book for me, including all those instances where I got the grammar wrong, even after all these years writing. For his input on the technical side, thanks to David Medinets who made sure what I wrote was correct and didn't go into so much detail that the readers would be scared off!

A big thanks as well goes to all the people who allowed me to include their modules on the CD, and especially to Larry Wall and Matthias Neeracher, who gave me permission to include Perl 5.6 and MacPerl 5.2.0r4 on the CD.

The penultimate thanks go to Neil Salkind, my agent, for finding me the book in the first place, and to the rest of the team at StudioB for keeping all my contracts, negotiations, and checks in order.

Finally, the biggest thanks should go to my wife for listening to my rants and raves when things weren't going well, and for letting me continue this writing lark.

Contents

Introduction

When Neil, my agent, approached me about the possibility writing this book, I initially thought it would be quite fun and easy. Imagine writing about all the cool Perl tricks people may not know about!

Then it seemed more difficult than I thought. I've been using Perl for more years than I care to remember, for everything from a few systems-administration tasks, to Web sites and even some pretty cool internal services for managing my time and the house.

My servers currently employ Perl to keep an eye on what's on TV—they download the information, store it in a PostGreSQL database, and report back to me. They also monitor the weather, using an electronic weather-monitoring system, again recording the information in a database—only this time it's MySQL, and it produces graphs, too. Another script gets the latest DVD releases, and I've even got a system that downloads a daily dose of all my favorite cartoons.

I download e-mail from my POP accounts and mail it to a special mailbox on my home network. Another script scans the latest topics and trends on newsgroups, and a separate set of scripts monitor my internal network and let me know when problems arise.

Other scripts let me update my Web sites easily, check my Web sites for errors, and even manage the services on a Windows NT server from a browser. I have a set of scripts that trawl through my Microsoft Word documents and extract the code elements so I can include them on a CD or place them on the Web site.

I've even got a suite of scripts that control my internal documentation archive. Being a writer and all-around computer enthusiast, I've got documentation on Perl, Python, PostScript, X, HTML, you name it. The scripts allow me to view any document on any topic, most of it generated dynamically. I can even search it all using yet another suite of Perl scripts.

The foregoing uses of Perl are routine to me. So I asked myself, "What do I select as topics to include in the book?" Then of course I knew. My usage of Perl might be natural to me, but it might not be to the readers; so I included some of my personal uses in the book and added a few others—including some that are completely new to me!

About Me

I've been playing with computers since I was about seven or eight years old, just at the point where in the United Kingdom the computer revolution was taking off with the Sinclair ZX80, ZX81, and later the ZX Spectrum.

More recently, I've worked at a few Internet companies and an advertising agency doing work for Digital, Raytheon, Oracle, and Hewlett-Packard. I've taught people at GCHQ and the BBC how to use the Internet and write Web pages.

For the last four years, I've been writing books, starting with one on porting Unix applications to the new BeOS operating system. I then moved on to *Perl: The Complete Reference* and both the Perl and Python Annotated Archives. I've also just finished a book on using the iMac; another on ActivePerl, the previously Windows-only version of Perl; and yet another on debugging Perl.

When I'm not writing or researching for my writing, I'm usually still playing with Perl (or Python), and the object of my play probably has to do with one of the aforementioned Perl services.

About This Book

It should be obvious by now what this book is all about, but just in case...

This book is an attempt to highlight some of the cool things you can do with Perl that you might not necessarily be aware of.

I've included scripts for a wide variety of topics, such as generating and playing music, the Web, networking, systems administration, and just a few obscure topics that you'd never think were possible with Perl at all. Most of the topics use an external module available on CPAN, but some use modules built into the standard Perl distribution, and others just use a technique or function in an unusual way.

For each topic I've explained the topic itself, the module, the technique used, and anything else I think relevant. The script is included on the enclosed CD-ROM, rather than reproduced entirely within the book.

Each of these sections contains several numbered items with step-by-step instructions for adjusting a specific configuration option or running an add-on program that will perform a specific action, such as making your screen look different or improving the performance of your mouse. You probably won't want to make every single one of the changes in the book, but you'll almost certainly discover plenty of things that will let you run Windows the way you want it, rather than the way Microsoft gave it to you.

What's on the CD?

◆ One or more scripts used to demonstrate the featured topic or technique for each number.

◆ Where possible, the module or modules required by the script. I've tried to obtain approval for all the modules, but for modules that I couldn't obtain approval for, information on where they can be downloaded is included instead.

◆ Where necessary, any sample data files.

◆ A copy of the latest stable (v5.6) of Perl.

◆ A copy of the latest version (v5.2.0r4) of MacPerl.

Unfortunately, due to licensing restrictions, we were unable to include a copy of the ActivePerl distribution for Windows, but you can download it from `www.activestate.com`.

The CD is organized according to each numbered tip in the book.

Conventions

Most of the book is formatted like this sentence. But occasionally a `function`, URL, or `file.name` is formatted with a fixed-width font as shown here. Some *variable names* are italicized. A few sections of

```
Code listing; #look like this.
```

N O T E Finally, I've occasionally included a note to highlight something of particular interest.

Contacting the Author

My Web site on www.mcwords.com contains details about all my books, including the latest version of any scripts, a list of any errata for a title, and much other information you might find useful.

Of course, if you find something wrong, please let me know so I can update the Web site. To contact me, either use the Web site or e-mail me at mc@mcwords.com.

Data Manipulation

I'll start the first section by looking at some data-manipulation and processing tools available, both within Perl and as CPAN modules. Although data manipulation is one of Perl's most basic features, it's also challenging. Data manipulation in Perl is not a simple case of extracting some information and formatting it as you like.

1 Storing Numbers in Less Space

```
vec
Built-in
www.perl.com
```

You will occasionally want to store information without taking up much space. For example, when storing information in a database where you have many types of numeric data, the temptation is to use a simple integer or character field to store a Boolean or integer value so you can determine different options and preferences. For example, you might use a Boolean field, set to "1" or "0," to record whether the user should be e-mailed. But the Boolean value would consume more space than storing the on/off value in a single bit of information.

Often the requirement for lowering memory usage is a lack of space to store the data—adding new information to a fixed-width data field is a good example. Sometimes, it's just the sheer volume of data that you want to store. When storing information in a physical file or database, you probably have little to worry about. But when compiling a report and importing the entire database into RAM, memory availability starts to become a problem. Perl is more than happy for you to allocate huge amounts of memory for parsing information, but the operating system may not be so willing to give you the memory you need.

Because Perl allows you to allocate such large amounts of memory, it's easy to forget how much space you are really using. A character is usually stored within a single byte, whereas an integer is stored within Perl as 32 bits, or 4 bytes. Thus, a single record with 10 options fields that only have one of four values will take up 10 bytes if stored as characters, 40 bytes if stored as integers. On a single record, it isn't much of a concern, but on 100,000 records that's a megabyte of information, or 4MB with integers, just for the sake of storing some simple on/off-switch information.

The solution is to compress the information that you want to store into a smaller space. Four different values can be stored in as little as two bits, so your 10 fields could be stored in just 20 bits, or less than 3 bytes. For 100,000 records, that reduces the storage space to about 292KB, just over a quarter of the uncompressed requirement.

Perl allows you to store very small integers into a scalar using the vec function. The most common usage for vec is in conjunction with the select function to pack in the bits for specifying the file numbers to be monitored. The function vec can of course be used for packing any integers into a smaller structure. The basic format for the function is:

```
vec(SCALAR, OFFSET, BITS)
```

SCALAR is the variable you want to store the information in, and Offset is the offset within SCALAR that you want the information to be stored or accessed from. The bit accessed depends on the value of BITS. For example, if you had 16 one-bit values to store, then option 13 would be at bit 13, or offset 12 (since references start at zero). On the other hand, with eight two-bit values to store, the following expression would access two bits, starting at bit 11:

```
vec($scalar, 5, 2);
```

BITS defines the number of bits needed to store the information. Care needs to be taken here to ensure you specify the right number of bits; too many and you waste space, not enough and you risk losing the information you want to store.

You use the function as normal to extract information from the scalar, using the parameters you supply to specify the location within the scalar for the information you want to access. When populating the scalar, you assign the function a value, just like any other variable. For example, you could populate a scalar with settings like the following:

```
vec($optstring, 0, 1) = $print   ? 1 : 0;
vec($optstring, 1, 1) = $display ? 1 : 0;
vec($optstring, 2, 1) = $delete  ? 1 : 0;
print length($optstring), "\n";
```

The length reported should be "1"—all three settings have been compacted into the one scalar, which should be only one physical byte in length.

The scalar is of course just a standard scalar variable, so you could populate it with any information and then use vec to extract it. For example, you could populate a scalar with a string and then get a single character from it, like so:

```
$scalar = 'Martin';
print chr(vec($scalar,3,8));
```

Note that you have to use chr, because vec returns a numerical value, not a character.

For the sample script included on the CD, I've created a simple program that records your current activity and then allows you to report on those activities, so you can see how you've spent your time. For example, to log yourself as being at a meeting, use this code:

```
$ vec.pl -a meeting
```

To determine the last time you recorded a particular activity, just run the script without any options:

```
$ vec.pl
At Fri May 12 16:03:24 2000: lunch
```

You can also specify multiple activities; for example, imagine you were at a project meeting that included lunch:

```
$ vec.pl -a meeting lunch project
```

To get a report of your activity, use the -r command-line option. It would produce a report similar to the following:

```
$ vec.pl -r
Tue May  9 16:04:52 2000: lunch, holiday
Tue May  9 16:04:57 2000: break (00:00:05)
Wed May 10 12:03:24 2000: lunch (19:58:27)
```

All the information is stored sequentially within a file as a packed structure. The first part of the structure contains the epoch offset for the time, and the second part has the byte that contains the activities.

I used the script for years as a way of tracking my time. It was a quick command-line entry, and it supplied a clear idea of what I was doing.

Because I worked on multiple projects, I was often updating this information every few minutes. So a traditional system would have used up voluminous space in very little time.

2 Creating Graphs in Perl

GD/GD::Graph
Lincoln Stein, Martien Verbruggen
stein.cshl.org/~lstein

Once you've developed a database or a parsing engine for taking information and reporting on its contents, you need to think about how you can display the information for it to be valuable to the user. You could use a fixed-width font to display information, using tabs to separate columns, or you could use an HTML table.

They say a picture paints a thousand words, and if that's the case, then the obvious solution—for data that warrants it—is to display the information as an image. Imagine you have a "build-to-order" system that lets a client specify a series of options in order to build a final product. Wouldn't it be nice to show the user what the final product looks like?

If you could generate a picture on the fly, then you could offer any sort of information in graphical format, increasing the chances of the information being understood. The GD module allows you to create pictures entirely within Perl.

I'll use the GD::Graph module to take book-sales-rating information and display it as a line graph. GD::Graph in fact consists of two scripts, and they are almost identical. The first script produces the graphic as a file and the second as an inline image for display within a Web browser, with the script acting as a CGI solution to the same problem.

The core of the script is really the GD module, which provides a generic interface within Perl for creating graphics files. The core library includes the methods necessary to draw lines and create basic shapes, such as circles and rectangles; the library also allows you to save the contents to a file.

N O T E The file types supported by the GD library are currently limited to an internal GD format and the PNG, or Portable Network Graphics format. PNG can be used with nearly all Web browsers, which have supported this format for many years, largely driven by the spate of court actions by Unisys, owners the LZW compression technology used in the GIF format.

The GD::Graph Module

For the script I'm using the GD::Graph module, which provides the base library for creating five basic chart types: lines, bar, point, linespoints, pie, and area. A sixth chart type, mixed, allows you to overlay more than one graph type within the same image. See the table for a description of the different graph types.

GD::Graph Type	Description
lines	The graph will be displayed as one continuous line, using the data points as anchor points between each line component.
bar	Bars are used to display the value of each data element.
points	The graph is displayed as a series of points, where each point represents the value of the data—no lines or bars are drawn.
linespoints	This combines the lines type with the points type and is most useful when you want to highlight specific values within a line graph or compare two or more data sets using a baseline and a series of points.
area	The area underneath the line represents the values of the individual data sets—think of area as a solid form of the lines type.
pie	Individual data points are displayed as a fraction of a pie, using the overall point value title to calculate the portion.

Each graph is represented internally as an object, so to create a new graph, you create a corresponding graph object, such as:

```
my $my_graph = new GD::Graph::lines();
```

You can also define the overall size of the image that is eventually created:

```perl
my $my_graph = new GD::Graph::lines(640,480);
```

The previous code will create an image 640 pixels wide and 480 pixels high. When the graph is drawn, the size of the individual bars and lines adjusts to fill the entire space given.

The options for the graph, such as the labels, division sizes, and titles, are initialized using the set function, which accepts a hash as a parameter. All aspects of the graph are fully configurable, so you can change everything from the label text to the frequency and separation of the tick marks used to display the y-axis. The more commonly used options generic to all graph types are shown in the following table.

Option	Description
t_margin, b_margin, l_margin, r_margin	The top, bottom, left, and right margins between the edge of the drawn graph and the canvas.
transparent	If set to 1, the background color will be set to transparent, useful for creating transparent backgrounds for Web graphics.
long_ticks	If set to 1, then the tick marks used to indicate each data point will be drawn at the same length as the graph width or height. Can be set on individual axis using the X_long_ticks and Y_long_ticks options.
y_tick_number	The number of ticks to be drawn on the y-axis. The default is 5.
x_label_skip, y_label_skip	This option sets the number of data points to skip when displaying tick marks on the axes. The data points themselves will still be plotted.
x_labels_vertical	Prints the x labels vertically, instead of horizontally.
x_label, y_label	The overall title for the x and y axes.
title	The title for the entire graph.

Usually the default options will work fine, but you may want to adjust the number of labels plotted on each axis to make the graph more readable. In addition, you can also control the fonts used to display the different aspects of the graph using a series of predefined font objects that tell the GD library how to render the text you supply into a graphic.

Once you've set up the graph and configured it to display how you like, you need to plot the data. The `plot` method accepts a reference to an array of arrays. For a line graph, which is what I've used, the first array contains the labels for the x-axis, and subsequent arrays hold the data values to be plotted on the y-axis. Because you can supply separate arrays of data, your table can display different data sets, overlaid on one another.

To write the graph out to a file, you need to call the `png` method on the GD object that is returned when you plot the data by calling the `plot` method. The method returns the binary data that makes up the graphical representation of your graph. This data is encoded in the PNG format, so you can use `print` to write the data to a file. In my case, I'll use the following:

```
open(IMG,'>file.png') or die $!;
print IMG $my_graph->plot(\@data)->png;
close(IMG);
```

To return the information directly to a browser, print to `stdout`; but change the normal HTTP header that you would return, as follows:

```
print "Content-type: image/png\n\n";
print $my_graph->plot(\@data)->png;
```

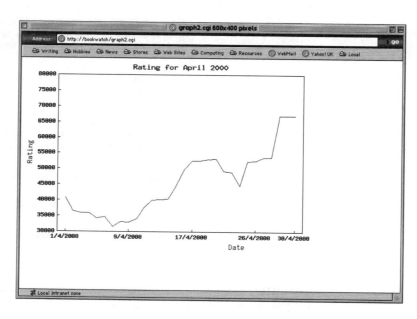

3 Using Minimal/ Maximal Matches

Any Regular Expression
Built-in
www.perl.com

Questions about Perl programming often relate to performing very specific text matches using regular expressions. For example, consider how HTML tags could be stripped from the following HTML code, leaving only the title text:

```
<font size="+1"><b>Title</b></font><br>
```

The solution most people new to Perl immediately opt for is the following regular expression:

```
s/<.*>//g
```

However, this expression removes everything from the entire line; the first angle bracket matches the first angle bracket in the line, and the second matches the last one in the line. Perl is here performing a *maximal match*— it's matching as many repetitions of the wildcard character as possible. Essentially, it matches everything until the closing angle bracket.

A quick solution to the maximal match might be to use an inverse-pattern match to select everything up to the right angle bracket. For example, consider:

```
s/<[^>]*>//g
```

This line of code will extract the information you want, but it's not an ideal solution in all instances and only works because you have an opposite character to match against. Large tags, for example, used when specifying images, links, or tables, could span multiple lines and would fail when matched with the previous expression.

A quicker and easier solution is to tell the regular expression to handle a *minimal match*. Perl then would select the first matching character it sees, rather than the last matching character in the string. To specify a minimal match, just use a single question mark after the quantifier; for example, you can rewrite the above substitution as:

```
s/<.*?>//g
```

It works on all the quantifier expressions, so you can perform minimal matches on multiple items or a specified number of items. The following table lists the maximal and minimal expressions and their descriptions.

Maximal	Minimal	Description
*	*?	Matches 0 or more items.
+	+?	Matches 1 or more items.
?	??	Matches 0 or 1 items.
{n}	{n}?	Matches exactly n times.
{n,}	{n,}?	Matches at least n times.
{n,m}	{n,m}?	Matches at least n times but no more than m times.

The script on the CD takes an HTML page and converts it into a text file, taking into account some basic HTML structures, such as line breaks and paragraphs. To use, just supply the name of the HTML file on the command line; the resulting file will be sent to the standard output:

```
$ html2txt.pl index.html
```

The script uses a combination of maximal and minimal matches in order to delete and, where necessary, convert different HTML tags into their text equivalent.

4 Parsing an Apache Log File

Apache::ParseLog
Akira Hangai
www.cpan.org

Apache, and in fact most other Web servers, produces two types of log files, the access log file and the error log file. The error file has a format, but it's not always entirely obvious. Because it also includes the errors reported to stderr by any CGI scripts, it can often include much unformatted (but still eminently useful) information about any problems with access to or elements of the site. I'll ignore the error log for the moment. For now I want to focus on the access log.

The access log has a very strict structure. It lists the HTML, graphics files, other downloads, accesses to any other resource on the site—in short, everything downloaded by a browser through the Web server is included in the log. The basic format of the log is as follows:

```
host ident authuser date request status bytes
```
The description for each of those elements is shown.

Field	Description
host	The fully qualified domain name of the client, or its IP number if the name is not available.
ident	The identity information reported by the client, if IdentityCheck is enabled and the client machine runs identd.
authuser	The user ID in the request, if the request is for a password-protected document.
date	The date and time of the request, in the following format: [day/month/year:hour:minute:second zone]
request	The request line from the client, enclosed in double quotes (").
status	The three-digit status code returned to the client.
bytes	The number of bytes in the object returned to the client, not including any headers.

A typical log will look something like the following:

```
198.112.10.4 - - [25/May/2000:10:45:33 +0100] "GET /archive/
test.cgi HTTP/1.0" 403 5397
198.112.10.4 - - [25/May/2000:10:45:33 +0100] "GET /img/
search.gif HTTP/1.0" 200 138
198.112.10.4 - - [25/May/2000:10:45:33 +0100] "GET /img/
reviews.gif HTTP/1.0" 200 150
```

```
...
/img/projects.gif HTTP/1.0" 200 149
198.112.10.4 - - [25/May/2000:10:45:33 +0100] "GET /img/ram-
bles.gif HTTP/1.0" 200 149
198.112.10.4 - - [25/May/2000:10:45:38 +0100] "GET /archive/
HTTP/1.0" 200 10610
198.112.10.4 - - [25/May/2000:10:45:38 +0100] "GET /img/dream-
host/rewards.gif HTTP/1.0" 200 602
198.112.10.4 - mc [25/May/2000:10:49:56 +0100] "GET /cgi/
search.cgi HTTP/1.0" 200 1025
```

I've trimmed the code for brevity, but you can see the basic information included in a typical file. The problem is not extracting the information—you can generally extract with a simple regular expression (see table for an element-by-element example) or even by just using split—the problem is the sheer quantity of information and how you want to summarize and report on it.

Element	Type	Log Element
^	Beginning of line	
(\S+)	Non-whitespace string	Host
\s+	(whitespace separator)	
(\S+)	Non-whitespace string	Identifier
\s+	(space separator)	
(\S+)	Non-whitespace string	Username
\s+	(space separator)	
\[(.*)\]	All characters enclosed in square brackets	Time
\s+	(space separator)	
"(.*)"	All characters enclosed in double quotes	Request
\s+	(space separator)	
(\S+)	Non-whitespace string	Result

Element	Type	Log Element
\s+	(space separator)	
(\S+)	Non-whitespace string	Bytes sent
$	End of line	

A typical log file for a garden-variety site will run a few thousand or perhaps a few hundred thousand lines. Large sites like Amazon and eBay get millions of hits every day! Once you've got the information, do you want to report hits per page, object, date, or time? If you want to report errors as well, it gets more complicated, as error logs can be made up of multi-line entries.

Although you could produce your own toolkit for parsing the logs, that's not what Perl is about. On CPAN you'll see a module called Apache::ParseLog. The module takes the access and error logs generated by Apache and parses them into an internal object structure that allows you to access summarized information through a series of hashes and nested hashes.

The Apache::ParseLog module reads the httpd.conf file to determine the location of the access and error logs. You then call object methods to get the information you need. For example, to get a report of the errors logged, ordered by date, you could program the following:

```
use Apache::ParseLog;
my($base) = new Apache::ParseLog('httpd.conf');
my($elog) = $base->getErrorLog();
my(%errorbydate) = $elog->errorbydate();
foreach (sort sortdate keys %errorbydate)
{
    print "Date: $_, Errors: $errorbydate{$_}\n";
}
```

The scripts on the CD produce a number of different reports, like simple error reports and reports by date, host, and page.

5 Reading and Writing Audio Files

Audio::Wav
Nick Peskett
www.cpan.org

I remember many years ago everybody was excited with the new Sinclair ZX Spectrum (the competitor to the Commodore C64)—it could play sounds! Now everyone takes audio for granted, and computers beep, whistle, play tunes, and even allow you to play electronically generated music.

But what if you want to produce and play some music from within Perl? Much better solutions for producing and playing music exist, but they are not anywhere near as much fun doing so within Perl.

Some Perl solutions make it easier. For example, the ever-useful CPAN has a MIDI module (by Sean M. Burke) that lets you communicate with an external MIDI device. (MIDI is short for Musical Instrument Digital Interface, although almost everyone just uses the acronym.) MIDI allows musical instruments to communicate and even control one another.

With a MIDI interface, you can control and sequence music electronically. Musicians can thus mix and play sequences together, probably using a synthesizer, without having to manually play the notes. Most computers with a soundcard (or Apple Macs with QuickTime v3.0 or greater) have the ability to act as MIDI synthesizers.

The main benefit to MIDI, as opposed to a digital music formats like MP3, AIFF, or WAV, is that a MIDI file only has to tell the synthesizer what notes to play. When you play a MIDI file, the soundcard (or QuickTime) produces a synthesized version of the sound, such as drum or piano. A MIDI file is therefore much smaller, since you're not actually recording/digitizing the sound.

The range of supported instruments and sounds is limited, however, and many have a synthetic sound that doesn't sound like the original. Furthermore, MIDI files require a suitable MIDI device. Even with built-in synthesizers the problem exists of reproducing a number of instrument sounds simultaneously—many support only four or eight, not quite enough for a full orchestra!

The other alternative is to generate your own audio file, by writing the raw audio to a WAV file and then playing it. You could even write direct to the audio device.

For the script on the CD, I've made use of the `Audio::Wav` module from Nick Peskett. The module provides the methods needed to write the raw audio data that makes up the WAV (Windows Wave audio format) file. WAV files consist of a sequence of waveforms that make up the tone, based on a particular frequency. It's a combination of the sampling frequency, sample rate, and the frequency that make up the tone. The tone should be in the form of a sine wave (hence Windows Wave audio format).

The sample script on the CD includes a function called `Write_note`, which takes the frequency (see the table), the duration (in seconds), and the sample rate and produces a data stream that represents that note and duration. You can then start to generate tunes within Perl, writing the information directly to a WAV file that you can then play with your favorite media player. The table gives a list of frequencies, based on the harmonics that A flat in the third octave has a frequency of 110Hz.

Note/Octave	$C_{,,}$	$C_{,}$	C	c	c'	c''	c'''	c''''
C	16.35	32.70	65.41	130.8	261.7	523.3	1046.6	2093.2
C#	17.32	34.65	69.30	138.6	277.2	554.4	1108.8	2217.7
D	18.35	36.71	73.42	146.8	293.7	587.4	1174.8	2349.6
D#	19.44	38.89	77.79	155.6	311.2	622.3	1244.6	2489.3
E	20.60	41.20	82.41	164.8	329.7	659.3	1318.6	2637.3
F	21.82	43.65	87.31	174.6	349.2	698.5	1397.0	2794.0
F#	23.12	46.25	92.50	185.0	370.0	740.0	1480.0	2960.1
G	24.50	49.00	98.00	196.0	392.0	784.0	1568.0	3136.0
G#	25.95	51.91	103.8	207.6	415.3	830.6	1661.2	3322.5
A	27.50	55.00	110.0	220.0	440.0	880.0	1760.0	3520.0
A#	29.13	58.27	116.5	233.1	466.2	932.3	1864.6	3729.2
B	30.86	61.73	123.5	246.9	493.9	987.7	1975.5	3951.0

If you want to play an audio file, try using the `Audio` module from Nick Ing-Simmons or the `Win32::Sound` module. For the latter, it's a simple case of:

```
use Win32::Sound;
Win32::Sound::Play("file.wav");
```

I'll leave it to the reader to discover why the script included on the CD is called `ceottk.pl`!

6 Playing Audio CDs

```
Audio::CD
```
Doug MacEachern
`www.cpan.org`

Did you know you can use your computer for playing audio CDs? I'm sure you probably did; people often check out the capability soon after getting a new machine. For good quality, though, you need to either have a decent set of computer speakers or pipe the output through a hi-fi. I've been unimpressed by the quality of MP3 (years of selling professional-quality audio components, I'm sure), and I sit at my computer within arm's length of my hi-fi, anyway.

But before I got my hi-fi, the only way I could listen to CDs in my study was through one of my computers. One limitation was that whenever I wanted to play a new CD or change tracks, I had to change over to the CD-playing application to eject the CD or push the tracking button. A second frustrating limitation was that I had to stop listening whenever I wanted to use the CD-ROM drive for data.

I opted to use one of my servers to play CDs, because I rarely used the server to do any work. But it was headless (i.e., without a monitor, keyboard, or mouse), so changing the CD or tracks became overly complex. The solution was to control my CD player remotely, such as via a Web page.

The `Audio::CD` script, the solution I found, works in conjunction with the `libcdaudio` library to provide a suite of functions to control the CD player on Solaris, SGI, and Linux machines. You can start and stop, play individual tracks, and skip over sections and entire tracks, all from within Perl.

I wrote a very quick script, which I used for some time and still do occasionally, that allows me to control the basic aspects of a CD player through a Web page. Further, the `Audio::CD` module allows me to obtain and display information from the CDDB audio database (see the sidebar). The CDDB database contains information on thousands of CDs, including the title and artist and, where relevant, information on individual tracks.

N O T E   The Web carries with it some limitations. It is pointless to offer a time-skip, for example, because it would take longer to redisplay the page than it would to skip!

CDDB

If you've checked the features of the CD player that comes with your machine, you've probably noticed that the software allows you to enter the artist, title, and track names for the CD. The information is recorded, so next time you insert the CD, the track and title information is immediately available to you again.

Surely, though, you're not the first person to have entered this information for the CD, right? CDDB (Compact Disk Database) tries to overcome redundancy. When you enter the title, artist, and track information, it can be sent to a central CDDB server, and then other people can download the information when they get the CD. Neat, huh?

But because CDDB is manually updated, you will sometimes find the information riddled with mistakes, or worse, just plain wrong. As an example, *The Best of Yazoo* is on the database as *The Best of Yaz*. Other than such mistakes, CDDB saves a lot of typing!

The mechanism for recognition is a combination of the number of tracks and individual track data (duration and unused storage blocks) to produce a unique ID. The ID is then stored as the key to the rest of the information. When you insert a CD, the track data is converted into the ID and then verified against the CDDB.

The Audio::CD module makes use of an object-based interface, which starts by getting the CD information, including the device and track data. Armed with that information, you can then call individual methods to play individual tracks. The system is so straightforward, you can start playing a CD in a single line:

```
use Audio::CD;
Audio::CD->init->play(1);
```

Other methods exist to stop playing a CD (stop), pause it (pause), and even eject the CD tray (eject).

To use information from the CDDB database, you first call the cddb method and then use the lookup method on the newly returned object to get the CDDB information:

```
use Audio::CD;
$cd = Audio::CD->init;
$cddb = $cd->cddb;
$data = $cddb->lookup;
```

You can then get CD information (title and artist) and individual track data by calling the appropriate methods. For example, the artist, title, and genre return the corresponding strings.

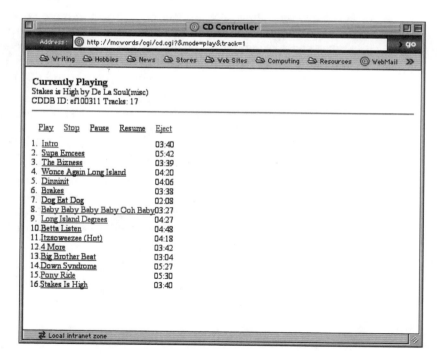

Installation Tips

When you've extracted the Audio::CD module, you'll find you need to download the libcdaudio library; you can download this library from cdcd.undergrid.net. You'll need to download and install the library before the Audio::CD module can be installed.

You might find that the first time you use it, the module fails to communicate with a CDDB server; thus you will end up with an empty track listing. Probably, the libcdaudio library hasn't initialized properly. You can get around the problem by using the cdcd application, also available at cdcd.undergrid.net.

The cdcd application also uses the libcdaudio libraries and provides a text CLI (Command Line Interface) for playing CDs. It also performs the initialization necessary to get the library working properly. All you need to do is run the application with a CD in the drive. The initialization first creates the necessary config file in the file .cdserverrc and then also creates the cache directory to be used to hold CD data. The cache stops your machine from connecting to the DB every time you ask for the information.

Finally, in order for the CGI script to work, you'll need to make sure that the library is able to find these files. Your Web server should be running as an anonymous user, so you can't simply redirect the libcdaudio configuration files to the user's home directory. Instead, as included in the script on the CD, the home directory and user environment variables are set with the information required by the libcdaudio library.

7 Handling PalmOS Databases

```
Palm::*
```
Andrew Arensburger
www.ooblick.com/software/coldsync/

In the eighties it was the Filofax, and in the nineties it was the Electronic Organizer. Now in the twenty-first century it's the PDA, Personal Digital Assistant.

Most people would be lost without it. It contains your names and addresses, calendar, and to-do lists; with the right software, it acts as your pathfinder, GPS (Global Positioning System) location tool, and your portable Internet terminal for e-mail and Web access.

But what if you want to work with information from your PDA while at your desktop machine? Most PDAs come with their own desktop software that provides not only backup capabilities but also synchronization with your favorite desktop organizer.

For some, though, it isn't enough. For a few months, I've been working on a project that needed a PDA version of a Web tool used for managing to-do lists. I didn't need to provide a Web interface for the Palm, which is what we were using, just a way of reading the to-do-list entries made by a user so that everybody could see their workload.

The PalmOS platform uses two file formats. The .PRC files are resource files that contain program information—i.e., the resources used to build up individual applications. The .PDB (short for Palm Database) files are the databases used by those applications, and it's the tododb.pdb file on your Palm that contains your to-do list. The Palm database format is very simple to understand if you look past the raw-binary format and instead think of the data in a more structured fashion.

I'll describe what the Palm::PDB module, and its associated database-handler modules, allows you to accomplish. At its simplest level, the Palm::PDB module lets you open a .PDB file and then access the information within just as if it were a hash reference. For example, to open your tododb.pdb file, you can implement the following:

```
use Palm::PDB;    # Handles the base format
use Palm::ToDo;   # Handles the ToDo list database format

my $pdb = new Palm::PDB;
$pdb->Load("ToDoDB.pdb");
```

All you need to do now is access the information within the file, using the $pdb scalar as a reference to a hash structure that contains all the information.

For a to-do list, the top level of the hash contains two pieces of information that you need in order to extract the to-do items. The first is a reference to an array of all records in the database. You can extract the array as follows:

```
@records = @{$pdb->{records}};
```

The @records array will contain an array of the individual record structures. Each record is actually another hash. The keys of the hash refer to individual fields of the to-do entry. You can see a description of these fields in the table.

Field Reference	Description
due_day, due_month, due_year	The due date of the to-do item, or "undef" if no due date exists
completed	True if the to-do item has been marked as completed
priority	The priority of the to-do item
description	The quick description for a to-do item
note	The note attached to the to-do entry. Note that this can be undefined
category	The category ID number

All Palm databases support a set of categories used to divide up data within the databases without resorting to a special field. This is the second piece of information you need to extract from the top level of the database file. Palm databases are unfortunately limited to 15 categories (category 0 means the record is "unfiled"), but they are unique for each database. So you don't have to use the same categories in your address list as you do in your to-do list, for example.

The following code gets you a list of categories:

```
@categories = @{$pdb->{appinfo}->{categories}};
```

The Appinfo is a special database tree that contains application-specific information. In this case it's a list of categories. The categories are listed in order, so you can use the returned category list as a reference for the Category field for the database record.

Armed with all this information, you can now read and report on it in a Palm database. The script on the CD lists the category, title, and due date for all the entries in a PalmOS to-do-list database.

The `Palm::*` modules also support many of the other standard databases on your Palm, so you can also read and update your addresses, calendar, and notes using Perl and the right module.

Incidentally, you can create records in any Palm database using the following:

```
$record = $pdb->new_Record;
```

The code creates a new record of a suitable type. For example, to create a new to-do entry all you have to do is populate the fields seen in the previous table and then make sure that you close and write the database correctly using:

```
$pdb->Write("newtodo.pdb");
```

You can get information on the fields that make up other databases by reading through the documentation that comes with the `Palm::*` modules.

8   Using SQL with Text Databases

```
DBD::CSV
Jochen Wiedmann
www.cpan.org
```

E-commerce is the buzzword at the moment. Developing any kind of complex Web site, and even some relatively simple ones, requires the use of a database. Many different databases are available on the market, from the free, but exceedingly capable, PostGresSql and MySQL engines to the commercial offerings of Filemaker, Access, SQL Server, Oracle, and others.

All such solutions offer a SQL-based query interface, which makes them largely architecture neutral when submitting a query. With some minor exceptions, a SQL statement executed on one database should work unchanged on another.

Two issues, however, can cause complications. First, for whatever reason you may not have a SQL database engine. Having a solution that allows you to use SQL features, but without the SQL engine, would certainly help development. Even though mySQL or PostGresSql are free, they still need maintenance and support, which a simple text file does not.

Second, you may need to access fairly basic textual information but want to use SQL-like queries to extract it. For example, when dealing with the data contained in a simple text-delimited file, you might want to pick out rows from the file based on the information contained within a specific field. You can do so manually with Perl, but it can be a pain to write a handler when a solution already exists. Alternatively, you could parse the text file manually, perhaps even reading the entire file into memory in order to extract the information you want, but that's a bit messy and would probably make for a more complicated script.

To solve both these complications, you can use the DBI module in combination with the DBD::CSV driver. The DBI module, short for *Database Interface,* is a generic interface driver for talking to different databases. The module provides the base functionality and extensions used to write queries and transfer information to and from a database driver.

The database driver is the real guts of the system. The driver sits between the DBI module and the database that you want to talk to. In this instance you'll be using the DBD::CSV driver, which allows you to use standard CSV (comma-separated values) text files as database tables. Other drivers are available for all major databases I've already discussed, and many other drivers exist for not-so-obvious choices. Even an ODBC (Open Database Connectivity) driver is available so you can talk to databases that support ODBC, from the standard SQL Server and Oracle up to mainframe databases like DB2.

Because you use the same module and the same basic interface (through DBI) between a database engine and your script, you can use the same queries and methods to access two completely different engines. For example, the code below extracts all the data from a database table, irrespective of what driver you're using:

```perl
my $sth = $db->prepare("select * from acronyms");
$sth->execute();
while(my $row = $sth->fetchrow_hashref())
{
    print "$row->{acronym}: $row->{expansion}\n";
}
```

When working with a CSV database, you'd need to prefix that code snippet with:

```
use DBI;
$db = DBI->connect("DBI:CSV:");
```

Note that it's the test string that you supply to the connect method that defines what DBD (database driver) you use. With the CSV driver, the tables you create and query become individual CSV files—one for each table. At the moment the engine doesn't support table joins, but it's still good enough for simple databases.

Alternatively, to access the same information from a table stored on a MySQL database, use the following:

```
use DBI;
my $dsn = "DBI:mysql:mydatabase";
       $dbh = DBI->connect($dsn);
```

The DBI kit hides the complexity and lets you get down to the basics of submitting SQL queries and getting back information.

Incidentally, another advantage of the DBI toolkit accepting the driver as a string is that you can choose the driver on the fly. For example, I use the following at the top of one of my applications to identify whether I'm on the test or production server:

```
if ($webhost eq 'bookwatch.mchome.com')
{
    my $dsn = "DBI:mysql:bookwatch";
    $dbh = DBI->connect($dsn);
}
else
{
    my $dsn = "DBI:mysql:database=bookwatch;host=sql ";
    $dbh = DBI->connect($dsn,'bookwatch','password');
}
```

The CSV file has a fairly basic format: individual fields are separated by a comma, and individual records by a new line. To ensure that the field contents don't get confused with other fields, and to allow the embedding of commas into fields, individual fields can be delimited with double quotes. Most software that supports the CSV format automatically inserts double quotes between fields. Double quotes within the data are escaped.

CSV is a common export format for most other database systems, and it's the preferred text-output format from Microsoft Excel. The DBD::CSV module excels—no pun intended—by reading the CSV format exported by Excel, without any modifications.

Because DBD:CSV reads the CSV format directly, it solves the aforementioned second problem—that of using flat text files but through a friendlier query interface. Now the next time someone gives you a report in Excel, you can work with it without having to jump through hoops or write a custom solution!

For the sample script on the CD, I've taken an acronym database originally held in a CSV file on a PC, which itself was exported from a database I'd been building on my Psion handheld computer! To use the database, just supply a list of acronyms you want to identify:

```
$ acro.pl AAMOF IYSWIM
AAMOF: As A Matter Of Fact
Not found: IYSWIM
```

To add an entry, use the -a option:

```
$ acro.pl -a IYSWIM if you see what I mean
```

To delete one, use the -d option:

```
$ acro.pl -d IYSWIM if you see what I mean
```

You'll need to supply the full expansion so that you don't delete the wrong acronym expansion.

Migrating from One Database to Another

The original problem—being able to develop SQL databases without a SQL engine—needs to be addressed. Although text databases are fine, it's likely that once your project reaches a production environment you will need to move the information from the CSV files into a real SQL engine, such as MySQL or Oracle. What's the next step?

The DBD::CSV module gets around the limitation of requiring a database engine during development. Individual CSV files make up the tables in the database, and you can use standard SQL statements to extract the information from the tables. Thus, you can practice and optimize your SQL queries without needing to talk to a SQL database.

Unfortunately, one limitation exists. At the moment the DBD::CSV interface doesn't support joins. So if you have a multitable query, you'll need a proper database, or you'll have to use two or more queries to get the information.

That limitation aside, the DBD::CSV provides a useful stopgap between your development work and a full-blown database. But what do you do when you finally are able to talk to a proper database?

Whereas the DBI module will ease the process of providing a database interface within Perl, differences between the database engines guarantee that not everything will work as expected. Here are some tips for making the process of moving from one DBD driver to another a bit easier:

◆ Check that the return value from a DBD module matches what you expect. The DBI module doesn't normalize all the error codes and values from all database drivers, so check the documentation specific to the DBD module.

◆ Write SQL queries as tightly as possible so as to remove ambiguity and reduce the return data set to only what you need. Also, don't rely too much on engine-specific SQL components, especially datatypes. Some engines support 20 to 30 different types for different pieces of information. In reality you could probably get away with the types listed in the "SQL Refresher" section later in the chapter.

◆ Don't rely on engine-specific features. Transactions are not supported by all engines, and other features like outer joins, triggers, and persistent sequences are not always available.

◆ Avoid making assumptions about what is available. Ensure that your script knows which database interface it's using.

The easiest way to get around the issues raised in the previous tips is to write an extra level of interface between your application and the DBI module. From that interface you can make decisions about which tools and tricks to use according to the database driver. For example, you could create a function called add_acronym that sits between your script and the DBI interface. If your database supports transactions, add_acronym would use them; but for databases that do not support transactions, the function would just supply the SQL statement without using transactions.

SQL Refresher

Not everybody is a SQL expert, so I've included here a very brief overview of the main SQL statements you can use to create, modify, and delete tables and rows. The following SQL commands should work with any database that supports a SQL interface, including the DBD::CSV driver.

Four main SQL statements can be executed on a SQL database: SELECT, INSERT, UPDATE, and DELETE. You might also want to use a fifth statement, CREATE, which creates new objects (such as tables and indexes) within a database file.

Select

When you want to extract information from the database, you use the SELECT statement. SELECT retrieves a set of rows and columns from the database, returning a dataset. The basic format of the SELECT statement is:

```
SELECT field [, field, ...]
FROM table
[WHERE condition]
ORDER BY field [ASC|DESC] [, field [ASC|DESC]]
```

The *field* is the name (or names) of the field(s) from the *table*. Because SELECT allows you to specify the individual fields from the table, you can avoid many of the problems normally associated with extracting data from a text database. Instead of ignoring the fields you don't want to access manually, you only select the fields you want. You can also specify an asterisk as the *field* name, and it will select all fields within the table.

The WHERE condition allows you to specify the conditions under which a row should be extracted. For example, to extract a specific acronym, you might use the following:

```
SELECT acronym FROM acronym WHERE acronym = 'AAMOF'
```

N O T E   SQL isn't case sensitive—except when you're searching a field. But it's common practice to specify the SQL components in uppercase and the lowercase components for field, table and other data names.

The Order By clause specifies which fields should be used to sort the information; you can also select either Ascending or Descending order. Remember that for numbers, ascending is lowest to highest, and for text it's A to Z.

INSERT

The INSERT statement adds a row of information to a table and has the following syntax:

```
INSERT INTO table
[(colname [, colname ] ... )]
VALUES (value [, value ] ... )
```

Table is the name of a table into which the data will be inserted, and colname and value are the field names and corresponding values that you want to insert into the table. The field names and values should obviously match to ensure that the information is inserted correctly. If, however, you are inserting data into all fields, you can omit the list of field names entirely.

To add a new record to your acronym database, for example, you might use the following SQL statement:

```
INSERT INTO Acronyms (Acronym, Expansion)
VALUES ('PDQ', 'Pretty Darn Quick')
```

Because you are creating entries in both columns you can simplify the statement to:

```
INSERT INTO Acronyms VALUES ('PDQ', 'Pretty Darn Quick')
```

Update

The UPDATE statement updates the information for one or more rows in a table. The syntax for UPDATE is:

```
UPDATE table
SET column=value
[, column=value ...]
[WHERE condition]
```

Column and value are the column names and values that you want to assign to those columns. If WHERE is included, the statement will only update those columns that match condition. The condition expression uses the same operators and syntax as SELECT. Note that if the condition matches multiple rows, all of the rows will be updated with the given information.

To modify the entry for IIRC in your acronyms database, for example, you'd program the following:

```
UPDATE Acronyms SET Expansion='If I Recall Correctly'
WHERE Acronym='IIRC'
```

Note of course that the code would update all of the IIRC entries in the table—you could supply a more specific statement to ensure you update the correct row:

```
UPDATE Acronyms SET Expansion='If I Recall Correctly'
WHERE Acronym='IIRC' AND Expansion='If I Remember Correctly'
```

Delete

The DELETE statement is essentially identical to SELECT, except that instead of returning a matching list of rows from a table, it deletes the rows from the database:

```
DELETE [FROM] table [WHERE condition]
```

The condition expression finds the rows to be deleted. The FROM keyword is only optional on some database drivers—check the documentation for more information.

To delete all the IIRC entries from the Acronyms table, for example, write the following code:

```
DELETE FROM Acronyms WHERE Acronym = 'IIRC'
```

You can also delete all of the rows in a table by omitting the search condition:

```
DELETE FROM Acronyms
```

Create

If you are developing a database system, you may need to occasionally build your tables programmatically with Perl. One major benefit of so creating databases is that you can transport an application to another machine and have the script create the tables it needs to operate.

Not all databases support the creation of database tables. Many have some constraints on what you can do with a CREATE statement. However, for those that do not face constraints, the basic format for a CREATE statement is as follows:

```
CREATE TABLE table
(field type[(size)]
[, field type[(size)] ...])
```

The *field* is the name of the field to be created in the table, and *type* and *size* define the field's type and width.

The valid data types depend on the ODBC driver you are using. Some generic types should work on most systems. See the table for a list of the field types that should be translated by most drivers into the local format.

Data Type	Size Specification	Description
Char	(x)	A simple character field, with the width determined by the value of x.
Integer	N/A	A field of whole numbers, positive or negative.
Decimal	(x,y)	A field of decimal numbers, where x is the maximum length in digits for the number and y is the maximum number digits after the decimal point.
Date	N/A	A date field.
Logical	N/A	A field that can have only two values, true or false.

To create a table that will hold the time information for a task, for example, write the following code:

```
CREATE TABLE groups (login char(20),
                     password char(10),
                     userlevel int,
                     emails int,
                     isbns int)
```

Text Manipulation

Text manipulation is one of Perl's strongest attributes. Perl provides built-in facilities to split, extract, and reconstitute text at a very basic level. These methods are well documented, so instead I'll concentrate on some of the object-based modules that allow you to create and parse more complex file formats such as RTF and PostScript, in addition to the more mundane HTML format.

9 Talking HTML

HTML::Element, HTML::TreeBuilder
Gisle Aas, Sean Burke
www.cpan.com

I doubt anybody could have predicted the explosion of the Internet at the beginning of the 1990s. The Internet had been around for many years, but it wasn't until Tim Berners-Lee developed the HTML (Hypertext Markup Language) text-tagging system that it really exploded.

Within Perl, producing HTML is not that difficult. You just need to use a `print` or `printf` statement to send the information to the filehandle destined to hold the HTML. (Better ways of handling the generation of HTML exist. See numbers 16 and 17 for more information.)

But what if you want to modify existing HTML? If you look at a garden-variety HTML file, you should immediately spot some problems with the more typical approaches. Consider the following:

```
<table>
<tr align="top">
<td><em>Name</em></td>
<td align="left">Martin</td>
</tr>
</table>
```

Imagine that you want to update those <td> tags so they include an attribute that sets the background color and moves the alignment to the right. You could use a regular expression to modify the file, but you'd have to modify in two or three stages to make sure you picked up the bare <td> and the tag with an existing attribute. If you ran into more complicated

HTML, then you'd need to update the regular expressions so they could handle the new HTML syntax.

What you need instead is a way of parsing the HTML source, dividing it into its constituent parts, and then modifying the tags on an individual basis.

Once again, the CPAN archives come to the rescue in the form of the `HTML::TreeBuilder` and `HTML::Element` modules. The modules provide an object-based interface for first parsing an HTML file and then modifying the individual tags (elements) of the file. The process is first to import and parse the source file:

```
$root = HTML::TreeBuilder->new;
$root->parse_file('source.html');
```

Once you have the file parsed, you can then find individual tags within the source using:

```
$elem = $root->find_by_tag_name($tag);
```

The code returns an element object, so if you use a loop you can iterate over all the tags that match $tag. Then you can set the individual attributes of the tag using:

```
$elem->attr($attr,$value);
```

The script on the CD accepts a source file, destination file, and the name of a tag to modify. The remainder of the arguments are extracted in pairs and used to define the attribute and value.

If the previous HTML were in a file called `Source.Html`, you could add alignment and background colors using the following:

```
$ cvhtml.pl source.html dest.html td align right bgcolor
\#000000
```

The code generates a file called `dest.html`, which contains:

```
<html>
<head></head>
<body>
<table>
<tr align="top">
<td align="right" bgcolor="#000000"><em>Name</em></td>
<td align="right" bgcolor="#000000">Martin</td>
</tr>
</table>
```

```
</body>
</html>
```

Besides the extra HTML added to turn the source into a valid HTML file, you can also see how the `<td>` tags have been modified, including changing the existing attribute from "left" to "right."

You can also use the same modules as a way of optimizing and cleaning the HTML you write, by removing spurious tags and extraneous whitespace (spaces, new lines, and the like) and ensuring that tags and elements are output in a standard fashion. The following script does so:

```
use HTML::Element;
use HTML::TreeBuilder;
my $root = HTML::TreeBuilder->new;
my ($source,$destination) = @ARGV;
$root->parse_file($source)
    or die "Couldn't parse source: $source";
open(OUTPUT,">$destination")
    or die "Couldn't output destination: $destination";
print OUTPUT $root->as_HTML(),"\n";
```

10 Checking Web Pages

LWP::UserAgent, HTML::LinkExtor
Gisle Aas
www.cpan.org

It is incredibly frustrating to fine-tune your Web site only to find out one of the links doesn't work. Trying to trace the problem is generally quite easy on a small site, but on a large site the process of tracking bad links can be quite significant.

You can resolve the situation as follows:

1. Download a page from the queue.

2. Extract the links.

3. Build a list of links that match the base URL for the site.

4. Add the matching links to the queue of URLs to be downloaded and parsed.

5. Go to 1.

Whereas the foregoing series of steps sounds tedious, Perl can help you out. The LWP (libwwwperl) library from Gisle Aas consists of a number of different elements that allow you to communicate with Web sites, extract the individual components of an HTML page, and build and manipulate the URLs used to refer to different elements.

The LWP::UserAgent module provides a very quick way of downloading a single Web page. The term User Agent describes any piece of software that gets information on behalf of the user from a Web site. In this case you'd use a suite of software that allows you, through Perl, to not only download specific Web pages, but also to postprocess those pages once they have been downloaded and extract the links and image references from the site.

The LWP system is very easy to use. The LWP::Simple module, for example, has a function called mirror that accepts just two arguments—the URL of the page you want to download and the name of the file to store the downloaded page. The module handles all the communication with the Web site and determines if it succeeded (the result code is returned as part of the call). For example, the following fragment will download my home page into the file index.html on your hard disk:

```
use LWP::Simple;
$rc = mirror("http://www.mcwords.com", "index.html");
```

Actually, the fragment goes one stage further. It checks the modification time on the local file and compares it with the modification time returned by the Web site for the page. The fragment only downloads the page (and by that I strictly mean the HTML, not graphics or other elements) if it's changed.

You can even download information from sites that use cookies for authorization:

```
use LWP::UserAgent;
use HTTP::Cookies;

$ua = LWP::UserAgent->new;

$cookie_jar = HTTP::Cookies::Netscape->new(
        File    => "$ENV{HOME}/.netscape/cookies",
```

```
            AutoSave => 1,
            );

    $request = HTTP::Request->new('GET',
                            'http://www.blackstar.co.uk');

    $cookie_jar->add_cookie_header($request);

    $response = $ua->request($request, 'blackstar.html');
```

The code I've reviewed here so far doesn't parse a downloaded file. That's where the HTML::LinkExtor module comes in. It extracts all the links from a page and can be configured to send the link information to a function. The LWP::UserAgent module can also be set to automatically call a function, passing that function the downloaded page. You can now rewrite the problem-solving sequence as:

1. Download the page from the queue using LWP::UserAgent.

2. Use HTML::LinkExtor to get a list of links.

3. Build a list of links that match the site.

4. Add the matching links to the download queue.

5. Go to 1.

Step 3 is handled by the URI module set, which, among other tasks, takes a relative page reference (e.g., /projects) and merges it with another URL in order to determine the real URL (e.g., http://www.mcwords.com/projects).

Step 4 you have to handle yourself, and step 5 is easily handled by embedding the whole sequence into a loop.

The final part of this process is to determine in step 1 whether the download of a URL completed properly. If it didn't, then you need to record the error and just move on to the next page in the queue. I handle this in the script included on the CD by using a hash that records not only the URL with the problem, but also the status and a record of which pages reference that page. To use the script, just supply a fully qualified URL to the script, such as:

```
$ cklinks.pl http://www.mcwords.com
```

Notifications about problems with my site are always helpful! Send me an e-mail at mc@mcwords.com.

11 Talking XML

XML::Generator, XML::Parser
Benjamin Holzman, Bron Gondwana, Clark Cooper
www.cpan.org, www.netheaven.com/~coopercc/xmlparser/intro.html

A difficult process for a programmer is to design the database to store the information for the application. Although some information lends itself well to a rigid structure such as a set of SQL tables, other data does not. It is frustrating to be blocked from doing something just because of a fairly simple formatting problem!

So what do you do? One solution is SGML. SGML (Standard General Markup Language) has been used for many years as a way of marking up textual documents in a more intelligent format than the raw text. The difference between SGML and its cousin HTML is that SGML allows you to define your own tags and how you want those tags to be handled. SGML is thus practical not just for marking up documents for display, but also for marking up the information and data stored within a document so it can easily be searched.

XML (eXtensible Markup Language) is a subset of SGML. While it follows most of the SGML system, some of the complexity has been removed in order to make it easier to use as a way of displaying and formatting information for the Web. The original design goals of the W3C consortium when developing XML were:

1. XML shall be straightforwardly usable over the Internet.
2. XML shall support a wide variety of applications.
3. XML shall be compatible with SGML.
4. It shall be easy to write programs to parse XML documents.
5. The number of optional features of the XML standard should be kept to an absolute minimum (preferably zero).
6. XML documents should be human-readable and reasonably clear.
7. The XML design should be prepared quickly.
8. The design of XML should be formal and concise.

9. XML documents should be easy to create.

10. Terseness in XML markup is of minimum importance.

For the most part, the consortium succeeded. XML is easy to use, create, parse, and understand, even when reading it in its raw format. The XML 1.0 specification has been set in stone with the formal ratification on February 10, 1998.

It's become clear over the past year that XML can also be used as a practical means of storing any type of information and can even be used to exchange information. If you take a humble contacts database, for example, exchanging data between your desktop contacts and those in Palm or other handheld organizers requires a certain amount of mental gymnastics. What do you do about the fields not supported by one database, and what happens if you have more than one e-mail address?

XML should hopefully get around the issues by supporting a set of extensible fields for a given contact. Each database can then make up its own mind at the time of import about what to use and what to ignore, and should even be able to modify itself to handle the data stored in the XML document. In all likelihood we'll probably see a move to a suite of applications that read an XML contact document directly—when you want to exchange the information between programs you would exchange the XML document. Then all the application would have to do is tag the data appropriately!

Creating XML Documents

So how do you get the aforementioned to work? An XML document is surprisingly straightforward because you design most of the tags yourself. For instance, you could render a contact database using XML tags as follows:

```
<contact>
    <name>Martin C Brown</name>
    <email>mc@mcwords.com</email>
    <company>MCwords</company>
    <title>MD</title>
</contact>
<contact>
    <name>Joe Foobar</name>
    <email>joe@foobar.com</email>
</contact>
```

The preceding code defines two contacts, with a number of fields each. Note that you don't have to be specific here—the information for Joe doesn't include any company details, and you don't even have to introduce blank entries. You could even add another level of detail (the company tag) so you could handle multiple contact details:

```
<contact>
      <name>Martin C Brown</name>
      <email>mc@mcwords.com</email>
      <company>
           <name>MCwords</name>
           <title>MD</title>
      </company>
      <company>
           <name>MCslp</name>
           <title>MD</title>
      </company>
</contact>
```

To generate the information, you could just use Perl's `print` function, but it's better to use a tool like the `XML::Generator` module that allows you to produce and format XML data in a structured fashion. For example, you might populate a contact file using:

```
use XML::Generator;
my $gen = XML::Generator->new('escape' => 'always',
                              'pretty' => 2);
my $xml = $gen->contact($gen->name('Martin C Brown'),
                        $gen->email('mc@mcwords.com'));
```

You're still only dealing with a raw set of information here, though—to search the file or to format it for the Web, you'll need to parse that XML document. That's covered subsequently. If the XML is converted to HTML, a Web browser can view it.

NOTE At the time of going to press, the only browser that was able to format raw XML data using a CSS (Cascading Style Sheet) was Mozilla, downloadable from www.mozilla.org. The capability will obviously be rolled into Netscape in due time, and it's already a planned feature for future versions of Internet Explorer.

Parsing XML Documents

The XML::Parser module provides the necessary functions for taking a raw XML document and parsing the tags. Unlike the HTML::Parser module in number 9, the XML parser provides a method for handling XML tags on a generic, rather than individual, basis. So you can progress through the tags sequentially without worrying about what they are. What you do is create a new XML::Parser object and then define a number of handlers that process a start tag, an end tag, and any raw data. Once configured, you just supply the XML or file that you want to parse. As each token is reached, the corresponding function handler will be called.

The simplified parsing process can be very quickly used to reformat information from XML to HTML. The script on the CD will take the XML contacts file and convert it on the fly into a formatted HTML document.

The core of the process is a hash that contains a list of XML elements and the formatting used to display them. The hash in the script from the CD looks like this:

```
my %elements = (
    'contact' => [{ tag => 'tr'}],
    'email'   => [{ tag => 'td', attr => 'align=left'},
                 { tag => 'b'}
                 ],
    'name'    => [{ tag => 'td', attr => 'align=right'},
                 ],
);
```

The script formats the individual records as rows in the table, the names as emboldened, and both fields as cells of the table.

Of course, it's up to you to decide how use the information contained within the files. If it's for data storage, you'll probably want to use a combination of the XML::Parser and XML::Generator modules in order to generate and parse the information you are storing.

XML's Future

XML's future looks very rosy. The W3C consortium is happy with the current standard and is working on the supporting the other standards, such as CSS for formatting and displaying the information.

The consortium is also working on new *ML-based standards such as SMIL (known as "smile"), which expands to Synchronized Multimedia Integration Language, a new method of providing multimedia content. The consortium is also looking at MathML, a standard for formatting mathematical expressions.

XML is also seen as a new method for solving age-old problems. The structured, but unrestricted, formatting services offered by XML will solve many more problems than simply storing contact information. Microsoft is already working to use XML as the format used to store Microsoft Word documents, rather than their current proprietary format. It's likely other companies will follow suit.

Plans are even underway to use XML as a way of storing raw information on a disk, instead of with the current disk formats like FAT and Ext2. Documents would then be stored not as raw data streams, but as chunks of XML.

Perl seems like an ideal language to process XML information. Perl is great at text processing (which is what XML parsing is all about) and also at handling complex information in structured format. In fact most XML applications store the XML file internally as a hash.

Plans are also in the works to make the XML tools a standard part of Perl, and it's likely that when Perl 6 comes around it will include XML facilities as part of the standard library.

12   Creating a Searchable Index

Martin C. Brown
www.mcwords.com

It's frustrating to visit a Web site you know contains much information and not find what you're looking for. Web sites need to be very well organized. Some Web sites offer a keyword-search facility that enables you to locate information from documents on the site.

Providing such a service on your own site can be slightly problematic; in fact, a whole new software business has developed that sells search engines for sites. Such search engines can be expensive, but a custom solution can be complex. How will the search be performed? What information should be included so that it can be searched? How should search terms not located be handled?

Many ways exist to create and search an index of words. (It need not apply just to the Web, of course.) You could allow manual searching through each file each time, create a quick index of words, or create a full cross-referenced index of words and locations.

A manual search is quite straightforward, but for formatted or otherwise organized text it is necessary to extract and understand the information as it is searched. The last option, a fully cross-referenced index, is what most Web search engines use. It enables you to search not only for individual words, but also multiple words and even phrases.

You will need to work out a number of other issues, such as what to do with highly repetitive words like "the" and "a." Will they be indexed, too?

The solution included on the CD uses a very simple index that matches words with individual files for a Web-site searching engine. I actually developed it as a quick solution for providing a search service on my own Web site. The system works using three separate elements:

◆ An exclusion database that builds and indexes words to be ignored by both the indexing and search system

◆ An index-creation script that reads all the pages and produces the index database

◆ A search script that checks the word-index database and the exclusion database for suitable words

Excluding Words

Do you know how many times the definite article "a" is used in normal conversation and writing? Or how about something less common such as "like"? On my Web site alone it's used 25 times—now imagine that on a larger site.

It's pointless to index such words; in all likelihood people won't search for them. For this reason you can build a database of excluded words. The script procexc on the CD builds such a database. You can use the sample excludelist file on the CD as the basis for the exclusion database, as in:

```
$ procexc excludelist searchdb.exc
```

The searchdb.exc file is used by the search script to build the list of words to exclude. Because the list is impossible to determine by a computer, you need to build the list yourself—the version on the CD provides a good spread, but will doubtless need editing.

Creating the Index

The index-creation script takes the base directory for a search, the prefix to be stripped from the file's path, and the location of the database to be created. It then progresses through the entire directory tree, opening each file, stripping the HTML, and then adding an entry in the database.

The database is in GDBM format, so information can be searched using a hash. The GDBM format is only supported under Unix, but you could use the SDBM libraries that come with Perl. The keys of the hash are the words, and the corresponding value is a list of files in which the word appears. At all times the word being indexed is checked against the exclusion database and ignored if there is a match. There's no limit to the number of the files that can be matched in this way. Each match is entered into the database; assuming the database has room, you should be fine.

For example, to create a database of the Web site stored in usr/local/http/webs/mcwords, you might use:

```
$ buildb.cgi /usr/local/http/webs/mcwords/ /usr/local/http/
webs/mcwords searchdb
```

The code creates the database searchdb, which is used by the search script.

Searching the Index

The actual search script is quite straightforward; it takes the information from a Web form, separates the list of words by spaces, and then searches the database for each of those words. The information on matched words is placed into a hash that contains the HTML page title and a count of the number of words matched from the original.

Armed with the hash, the script then outputs an ordered list of those matches, from highest number of words matched to lowest, giving the title and URL required for the page on the site.

The solution is very simple and not particularly advanced or clever, but it does give any site the basic ability to support a searching mechanism. See the sample search output in the following graphic.

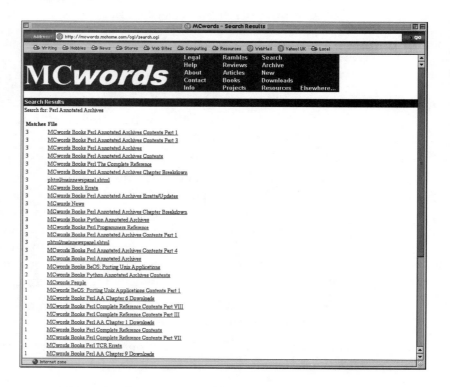

13 Searching/Replacing Text Information

Built-In Module
`www.perl.com`

Here's a feature so often ignored by Perl users you'll be amazed how useful it can be. Most Perl users never take the time to become familiar with its command-line options. This is a shame, because Perl hides some clever features there.

If you're like me, you probably spend much time programming, administering, and otherwise playing on Unix machines. Fairly often, you probably find yourself using tools like grep and sed to perform simple searches and conversions on text files or text data. The problem is that they don't easily interchange information, and if you want to perform a number of searches or replacements, the tools quickly become cumbersome. They also aren't supported by all platforms.

Did you know you could use Perl for that? I don't mean writing a script that opens a file, works through each line, and then outputs any matching entries. I mean using Perl's regular expression engine to search for and print out the selected lines from a file, or even to replace text within a file. Three ways enable you accomplish the simple searches and conversions: -n, -p, and –i command-line options.

Using Perl for Searching

The easiest way to quickly execute a single Perl statement is to use the -e option on the command line:

```
$ perl -e 'print 45+67,"\n"'
```

You might think that if you want to search a file you'd have to write a script to open the file and read its records, which you would then report on. With multiple files, it would get even more complex.

However, Perl supports the -n command-line option, which effectively puts the following loop around your script:

```
while(<>)
{
#Your script
}
```

The same loop iterates over each file supplied on the command line. However, no way exists of actually determining the filename, so it's only really of any use for searching within a single file. Because the script is automatically placed into the loop you'll need to use Begin and End blocks.

The script you write can do anything you like. The $_ special variable is populated with each line from the file, which means you can run complex regular-expression searches. For example, the following script will search a given file for the regular expression supplied as the first argument:

```
#!/usr/local/bin/perl -n
```

```
BEGIN { $search = shift;}
print if (m/$search/);
```

The shift in the BEGIN block takes off the first argument, while the rest of the script is embedded in a loop that opens each file on the command line. For example, you could use the script to pull lines out of a file that match either "Bob" or "Ethel":

```
$ perl mysearch.pl (Bob|Ethel)
```

Or you can be more adventurous and write a script that very quickly outputs a count report from a Web log:

```
#!/usr/local/bin/perl -n

BEGIN { %stats; }

($key) = ($_ =~ m/GET (.*?) HTTP/);
$stats{$key} = 0 unless(exists($stats{$key}));
$stats{$key}++;

END
{
    foreach $key (sort { $stats{$b} <=> $stats{$a} } keys
%stats)
    {
        print "$key: $stats{$key}\n";
    }
}
```

Now all you have to do is set the permissions on the file to "executable" (using chmod) and then, to get a report, type:

```
$ quickwl.pl access.log
```

The -p option is identical to the -n option except it also automatically prints the line to stdout, effectively placing the following script around your code for each file opened on the command line:

```
LINE:
  while (<>)
  {
  # Your script
  }
  continue
```

```
        {
            print or die "-p destination: $!\n";
        }
```

The -p option can be useful in situations when you want to preprocess the input line before it is displayed on the screen. For example, the following code very quickly changes colons in a file to vertical bars:

```
#!/usr/local/bin/perl -p
s/:/|/g;
```

You can rewrite the code on the command line as:

```
$ perl -p -e 's/:/|/g;' /etc/passwd
```

Using Perl for Replacing

Although the ability to search is quite useful, you can also use Perl's command-line options to directly search and replace information in a file. Other ways exist of doing so, such as using sed or an editor, but with Perl you can not only script the process, you can script it for a bunch of files.

Here, use the -i command-line option. It forces Perl to perform an "in-place" edit, which means instead of writing the file content to stdout, the information is written back to the opened file. (In actual fact it writes the information out to a new file and then replaces the old one with it.)

Furthermore, you can add an extension to the -i option; thus, -i.bak renames the original file to have a .BAK extension and then writes the new file to the original filename. For example, to update the earlier code that printed out a reformatted version of the /etc/passwd file, you could change (and break!) the delimiters using:

```
$ perl -pi.bak -e 's/:/|/g;' /etc/passwd
```

The code changes the file from using colons to pipe symbols, with the previous version in /etc/passwd.bak.

In code, what the -i actually does is:

```
$extension = '.bak';
LINE: while (<>)
{
    if ($ARGV ne $oldargv)
    {
        if ($extension !~ /\*/)
```

```
            {
                $backup = $ARGV . $extension;
            }
            else
            {
                ($backup = $extension) =~ s/\*/$ARGV/g;
            }
            rename($ARGV, $backup);
            open(ARGVOUT, ">$ARGV");
            select(ARGVOUT);
            $oldargv = $ARGV;
        }
        # Your script
    }
    continue {
        print;
    }
    select(STDOUT);
```

I'll go over a specific example. The following code is designed to renumber the user ID field in a passwd file; 1000 to 2000 will instead be in the range 9500 to 10500. The old file will be renamed to passwd.bak and the new passwd file will have been created:

```
#!/usr/local/bin/perl -pi.bak

@fields = split /:/;
$fields[2] = $fields[2] - 1000 + 9500
    if ($fields[2] >= 1000 and $fields[2] <= 2000);
$_ = join(':',@fields);
```

Here's another example. You can replace tabs with four spaces in an entire directory tree:

```
$ find . -type f | xargs perl -pi -e 's/\t/    /g'
```

Not only is the method quicker and simpler than using sed or a shell script, it also means you can perform more complex conversions. Again, the element of the script that you write is embedded into a loop, so you can do just about anything!

14 Generating RTF Files

RTF::Document
Robert Rothenberg
www.perl.com

Despite the increase in popularity of HTML and XML technologies for storing formatted document data, most word-processing programs still use their own proprietary formats (actually, future versions of Microsoft Word will use XML).

"Compatible" formats, however, have always existed. They allow you to exchange files between word-processing programs without losing too much of the formatting and style information. RTF, or Rich Text Format, is just such a file format.

RTF actually works in a very similar fashion to HTML; it's basically a text-based format, but it uses tags in the form of \tag, so embedding a piece of bold text is as easy as:

```
\b Some bold text \b
```

The RTF::Document module provides a more pragmatic way of introducing RTF elements and building them into RTF documents than producing the individual elements yourself.

I've used RTF (but not the RTF::Document module) in the past as a way of producing a formatted document based on data extracted from a database. The system was a time-reporting database used for project management, and it would produce an RTF document for invoices and orders that could then be checked and printed onto letterhead.

Because the document generated already had the correct fonts and styles, often the only modification required was the insertion of a note or a change to the description of individual items. Being RTF, I could not only open the document in Microsoft Word but also in Lotus AmiPro/WordPro, and I could even send it to suppliers and clients without worrying about whether they could read the generated document.

Before I look at the specifics of producing RTF documents, however, it's worth looking at the basics of any word-processed document. Most documents are based on a number of styles that define the attributes of a particular block of text. Attributes include the font, size, color and alignment of a particular section. You can define a number of fixed styles that can then be used elsewhere in the document without having to manually set each attribute. You can also manually configure individual words and characters with their own unique attributes.

To create an RTF document in Perl, you first start with an RTF::Document object. The RTF document standard uses the same basic principles as XML when used with a stylesheet—you must define the fonts and styles you expect to use in your document. The fonts and styles are then used to format the text as it is introduced into the document. For example, to set a new font, you could code the following:

```
my $rtf = new RTF::Document({
    doc_page_width => '8.5in',
    doc_page_height => '11in'
    });
my $font_mono = $rtf->add_font("Courier",
                { family => 'monospace', pitch => 'fixed',
                  alternates=>["Courier New", "Geneva"]
                } );
```

The first parameter to the add_font method is the name of the font you want to use. The second argument should be a hash reference that contains information about the alternatives that could be used if the font name you supplied isn't available.

In the table you can see a list of the different elements you can add into an RTF document.

Element	Method	Description
style	add_style	**Adds a style to the stylesheet, incorporating the font, size, color, and whether the style affects the whole paragraph or just the selected text.**
text	add_text	**Inserts formatted text, according to the supplied style and/or attribute settings supplied.**
-	add_raw	**Adds raw text to the RTF document. It can be used to insert RTF artifacts not supported by the** RTF::Document **module.**

Element	Method	Description
color	add_color	**Adds a color specification to the RTF document. Colors can be specified either using a string, such as "black," as levels of gray using a hash key of "gray" and a percentage value, or using a hash that defines the individual components of "red," "green," and "blue."**
font	add_font	**Adds a font to the RTF document. Note that fonts must be defined before used. A font is composed of its name, font family, and any substitutes you are willing to use.**

To introduce a piece of text into the document object, you could code the following:

```
$rtf->add_text($rtf->root(),
               { font_size => "20pt", },
               "$subject\n");
```

The first parameter refers to the location within the document that you want the text to be written—in this case, it's the root, or main portion. The third argument is the text of the paragraph. The hash contains the definition about how the next section of text should be formatted. In here you can specify a style, font, size, emboldening, underlining, and so on. Most options take a reference to another RTF object, such as a font or color; others take a raw specification, defined using a hash.

Some also have special options. For example, the underline attribute allows for a simple 0 or 1 to turn it on or off. It also allows for the string "continuous" so that spaces within the text are also underlined. (The normal operation is to skip spaces when underlining text.) The following example illustrates continuous underlining:

```
$rtf->add_text( $rtf->root(),
                { bold=>1, underline=>continuous },
                "Bold/Underlined Text\n\n")
```

The RTF::Document module performs all the work of inserting the necessary RTF formatting, and it also automatically inserts new paragraphs when it sees a new line in the inserted text.

Once you've finished adding all the elements, just call the `rtf` method to emit the RTF text, as follows:

```
print $rtf->rtf();
```

The information returned is just a string with RTF formatting; to save, you could easily redirect the output to a file. Once the text has been produced, you should be able to just open it within your favorite word processor to get a formatted version of the text.

The script I've included on the CD, `cv.pl`, takes a raw e-mail message and very simply formats it so that it can be "pretty printed" from your word processor.

15 Writing PostScript

PostScript::TextBlock
Shawn Wallace
www.as220.org/shawn

If you stop and think about the computer you're using now, it's amazing to consider how old the system and technology really is. Technology hasn't really changed that much: computers have become faster, users get more features each year, and the rules of Moore's Law still hold (see the sidebar), but essentially you're still using the technology and methods invented by Charles Babbage in the nineteenth century.

MOORE'S LAW

In the late 1970s, Gordon Moore looked at the advancing chip-making capabilities at Intel and proposed that computer technology would double in capacity every 18 months.

Although PostScript was developed in 1985, and is in its third incarnation at the time of this writing, little has really changed about the language. PostScript is still the leading standard used by everybody from the man in the street to the billboard printers. Most laser printers include a PostScript interpreter, and it's a useful universal format. So if you produce a Post-Script document, you can print it on any compatible printer or use one of the many tools, such as Ghostscript from Aladdin Systems, Inc. (see `www.cs.wisc.edu/~ghost/` for more information), to view the file on screen. PostScript's fine attention to detail and top-quality output (when coupled with a suitable printer) make it a great choice.

PostScript allowed designers to describe very precisely the location in which they wanted to print a certain element. Beyond the basics of page layout, PostScript also allowed dynamic scaling, which means you can take a font and scale it from 1 pt to 144 pt or more without any jagged edges. Likewise, line drawings can be easily scaled with the same quality.

I've used PostScript to output forms and charts dynamically generated from a database, without requiring the information to be translated or viewed from a client. By printing a PostScript file directly from the server, I had much better control over printing and queuing, and I could choose the right printer for the job.

The only problem with PostScript is that it's fairly complicated to program—I certainly don't recommend it for the casual programmer or even the experienced one. The language uses a stack for parsing data, and a simple mistype or missing command can render the file useless. Much "preamble" is generally required to set up the document detail.

You also have to be very specific about what you are printing. The page within PostScript is defined in terms of points—1/72 of an inch—and coordinates are mapped from the bottom left corner of the page. To print a simple piece of text on a page, you have to move the cursor to the location and then supply the text and "show" it. For example, the fragment below moves the cursor, selects a font, and then introduces some text:

```
0 setgray 20 672 moveto
/CenturySchL-Ital findfont
24 scalefont setfont
(Hullaballo in Hoosick Falls.) show
```

It's up to you to ensure that the text doesn't overlap. If you want to print another line, you'll need to calculate the size of the text that was printed, taking into consideration the size of the font. You'll also have to calculate how much space to leave between the previous line and the next, and you'll have to do the moving of the cursor yourself.

If you want to do something as complex as fully justifying the text, then you'll also have to place each word individually, determining its size and the spacing between each word. The specificity isn't required, but it does make the difference between a good document and an excellent one.

It is of course the preciseness and freedom with which you can place text and graphics on the page that makes PostScript so popular with design professionals. PostScript is just a text file; there's nothing special about the file format, so you could easily manually produce the file entirely within Perl. But Perl has a module for just about everything, and PostScript is no exception.

The PostScript module set provides a simple but effective way to produce the PostScript code. At its heart is the PostScript::TextBlock module. The module allows you to create a new block of text, formatted using a specific font, which can later be rendered into a final PostScript page.

To produce a document, you first need to create a new PostScript object:

```
$object = new PostScript::TextBlock;
```

Once created, you add text blocks using the addText method:

```
$tb->addText( text => "Monthly Report.\n",
              font => 'CenturySchL-Ital',
              size => 24,
              leading => 100
            );
```

The method requires one argument, the text to be printed, and the remaining arguments allow you to specify an alternate font (from the default), size, and leading (the amount of blank space between lines within a given block).

Because the module must know the size of the text to be placed, you should choose a font supported and recognized by the PostScript::Metrics module. Check the module documentation for details on the fonts supported.

Most printers have a default set of fonts built in, and further fonts can be loaded. But the module doesn't handle the use of fonts beyond those it defines because the module uses the font metrics to determine when paragraphs should be split into individual lines. If the interpreter (usually your printer) cannot find the font, then it'll substitute an alternative. But because of the way PostScript works, it's unlikely to result in a nice document.

Once you've finished adding all the text blocks, all you need to do is write out the information using the Write method. Write formats and returns the necessary PostScript to generate the pages. It calculates line widths and character spacing in order to produce the final pages.

The method accepts four arguments: the page width and height (in points), and the offset (remember, from the bottom left corner) of where to start. The following is an example:

```
open OUT, '>psoutput.ps';
my ($code, $remainder) = $tb->Write(572, 752, 20, 772);
print OUT $code;
```

The code returns an entire section (usually a page) according to the information supplied. It also returns a new textbox object that contains any remaining text. You'll need to issue a loop if you want to process more than one page. You'll also need to embed PostScript tags, which identify the individual pages and force the page to be rendered. PostScript uses the showpage function to embed the tags. You can get more information on the PostScript language from www.adobe.com.

So, for each page you'll need to call the following:

```
my ($code, $remainder) = $tb->Write(572, 752, 20, 772);
print OUT "%%Page:$pages\n";
print OUT $code;
print OUT "showpage\n";
```

To get an idea of the sizes of different page types, see the table, which lists sizes in points.

Paper Size	Width, Height
Letter	612, 792
Legal	612, 1008
Ledger	1224, 792
Tabloid	792, 1224
A0	2384, 3370
A1	1684, 2384
A2	1191, 1684

Paper Size	Width, Height
A3	842, 1191
A4	595, 842
A5	420, 595
A6	297, 420
A7	210, 297
A8	148, 210
A9	105, 148
B0	2920, 4127
B1	2064, 2920
B2	1460, 2064
B3	1032, 1460
B4	729, 1032
B5	516, 729
B6	363, 516
B7	258, 363
B8	181, 258
B9	127, 181
B10	91, 127
#10 Envelope	297, 684
C5 Envelope	461, 648
DL Envelope	312, 624
Folio	595, 935
Executive	522, 756

Once you've got the generated PostScript, you can write it out to a file (as shown previously) and then just send it to your printer, or you can use Ghostscript or another display PostScript solution, such as Solaris's dps.

It's hard to improve upon the example provided by the author, Shawn Wallace, in the toolkit—it should give you enough information to be able to write your own solution.

I have for some time been developing an HTML to PostScript converter, but I've got a long way before finishing—even with Shawn's code, there's still a lot of hard work to go!

CGI Tricks

Did you know that Perl is one of the most commonly used languages for Web development? The reason is quite simple: it's superb at processing the sort of text information that comes from Web browsers. Perl's also great at talking to databases, too. So not only can it get information from the browser, but it can also search, format, and display it back with ease. And you don't have to compile between each revision!

16 Using the CGI Module to Write HTML

```
CGI
Built-in
www.perl.com
```

Most people are aware of the CGI module as a way of parsing HTML form information and making it available within Perl either through an object interface or a simpler functional interface. What many people don't realize, however, is that the same module can also be used to generate the HTML in the first place.

So at a base level, simple operations, such as outputting headers and the formatting of individual sections of text, become much easier. At a more complex level, you can use the module to generate clean HTML that works on a particular vendor's browser.

One issue the CGI module addresses is that of complexity. Normally, when you want to produce HTML, you use a simple print statement and some suitable text. But it is prone to problems because you only have to mistype a tag name or the angle brackets, and the HTML produced is useless. By using a set of functions to generate the HTML, like those supplied by the CGI module, you eliminate most of those problems before you've started.

The module provides two methods for generating HTML: an object-based method that works with the object-based browser interface, and a simpler functional interface. Both methods use the same functions, and each function is named after the HTML tag it represents. For example, the following creates a "Hello World!" page using the object method:

```
use CGI;

$page = new CGI;
print $page->header,
      $page->start_html('Hello World!'),
      $page->h1('Hello World!'),
      $page->end_html;
```

You can achieve the same result with the functional interface as follows:

```
use CGI qw/:standard/;

print header,
      start_html('Hello World!'),
      h1('Hello World!'),
      end_html;
```

The latter code imports the standard set of functions from the CGI module and outputs the header, consisting of the content-type information that must be output to the browser; the HTML preamble; and the piece of text formatted using the <H1> HTML tag. It then closes the page. The text generated by the script follows:

```
Content-Type: text/html; charset=ISO-8859-1

<!DOCTYPE HTML
        PUBLIC "-//W3C//DTD HTML 4.01 Transitional//EN"
        "http://www.w3.org/TR/html4/loose.dtd">
<HTML LANG="en-US"><HEAD><TITLE>Hello World!</TITLE>
</HEAD><BODY><H1>Hello World!</H1></BODY></HTML>
```

You can see from the example that the H1 function accepts an argument—the text to be formatted—and that the resultant HTML includes the necessary start and end tags. The start_html function does the same basic operation, except the accepted argument is used as the <title>-tag text for the page title.

Other tags work in a similar fashion, and tags that accept multiple arguments are populated using a hash. For example, when creating a form, you can supply the method and action arguments to the tag by supplying a suitable hash, as shown:

```
print startform(-method => 'PUT',
                -action => '/cgi/mycgi.cgi'),
      textfield('roman');
```

Note that the action defaults to the name of the CGI script. You probably only need to explicitly define the script name if it's a different script from the one generating the form. I've also added a text field in the foregoing example.

The sample script on the CD provides a quick way of converting a sequence of Roman numerals, like those seen at the end of TV programs, to a decimal. The script uses the CGI module to generate HTML and pass the information returned by the form.

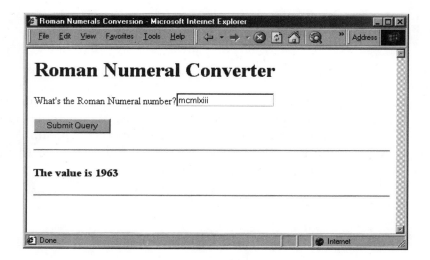

Export Sets

The CGI module doesn't export all of its symbols by default. Instead, it uses a series of import sets than define a set of functions to be exported. These are divided into sets of supported HTML tags, such as HTML 2.0 and HTML 3.0, and the core functions used to parse and supply parameters and other information. In the table you can see the import sets and the list of functions (and therefore HTML tags) exported.

Import Set	Exported Symbols/Symbol Sets
html2	h1 h2 h3 h4 h5 h6 p br hr ol ul li dl dt dd menu code var strong em tt u i b blockquote pre img a address cite samp dfn html head base body link nextid title meta kbd start_html end_html input select option comment
html3	div table caption th td TR Tr sup Sub strike applet Param embed basefont style span layer ilayer font frameset frame script small big
netscape	blink fontsize center
form	textfield textarea filefield password_field hidden checkbox checkbox_group submit reset defaults radio_group popup_menu button autoescape scrolling_list image_button start_form end_form startform endform start_multipart_form isindex tmpfilename uploadinfo url_encoded multipart
cgi	param path_info path_translated url self_url script_name cookie dump raw_cookie request_method query_string accept user_agent remote_host remote_addr referer server_name server_software server_port server_protocol virtual_host remote_ident auth_type http use_named_parameters save_parameters restore_parameters param_fetch remote_user user_name header redirect import_names put delete delete_all url_param
ssl	https
cgi-lib	readparse printheader htmltop htmlbot splitparam
html	html2 html3 netscape
standard	html2 html3 form cgi
push	multipart_init multipart_start multipart_end
all	html2 html3 netscape form cgi internal

17 Better Table Handling

CGI
Built-in
www.perl.com

One of my own personal bugbears when writing HTML is how HTML tables work. The basis is right—tables are split into table rows (the <tr> tag) and table cells (the <td> tag). But problems can arise as the table gets more complex and you add more tags and other elements. Missing a tag is generally OK, until you start to use tables embedded in tables, at which point the formatting fails. Forgetting to add a closing </table> tag will also cause the entire table to be ignored by the browser.

The solution is straightforward—use a function that puts the tags around a piece of text, as follows:

```
print td("Name"),td("Martin");
```

The CGI module provides this functionality for you. The real advantage of the CGI module, though, is that the function calls for creating table cells and rows and other multitag components, like lists, can be nested and therefore called more simply.

Basic Components

When you want to introduce a list into your HTML, you can create a multi-item list just by supplying a reference to an array of list items to the li function, as follows:

```
use CGI qw/:standard/;
print li(['Martin','Sharon','Richard','Julie']);
```

The code correctly produces the following HTML:

```
<LI>Sneezy</LI>
<LI>Doc</LI>
<LI>Sleepy</LI>
<LI>Happy</LI>
```

All you have to do is supply the <ul> or other list tags to define the type of list.

For table components the same rule applies. The following call generates three table cells with the correct start and end tags:

```
td(['Foxtrot', 'no', 'no' ]);
```

You can also supply attributes to the td tag by supplying a hash of the attributes and values as the first argument. To center the text in each of those cells, write the following code:

```
td({-align => CENTER}, ['Foxtrot', 'no', 'no' ]);
```

It generates the HTML shown:

```
<TD ALIGN="CENTER">Foxtrot</TD>
<TD ALIGN="CENTER">no</TD>
<TD ALIGN="CENTER">no</TD>
```

Obviously, the method is much quicker than either manually generating the HTML or making individual calls to the td function to generate each cell. It also ensures that the HTML is valid—the HTML tags are started and completed, and the attributes are properly quoted.

Nesting Components

Going back to the list example, to produce a bulleted list you can embed the call to li in a call to the ul function:

```
use CGI qw/:standard/;
print ul(li(['Martin','Sharon','Richard','Julie']));
```

It correctly produces the HTML shown:

```
<UL>
<LI>Sneezy</LI>
<LI>Doc</LI>
<LI>Sleepy</LI>
<LI>Happy</LI>
</UL>
```

Again, the format applies to table generation. You can embed a call to the td function in a call to Tr to build up the rows of a table, and the Tr function call can be embedded into a table function call to produce an entire table. For example, consider the following code:

```
print table({-border => 1},
            caption('Cartoons'),
```

```
         Tr({-align => CENTER,-valign => TOP},
            [th(['Toon', 'Download','Archive']),
             td(['Dilbert',      'no', 'yes' ]),
             td(['Foxtrot',      'no', 'no'  ]),
             td(['Grand Avenue', 'yes',' yes'])
            ]
         ));
```

It generates the following HTML:

```
<TABLE BORDER="1">
<CAPTION>Cartoons</CAPTION>
 <TR VALIGN="TOP" ALIGN="CENTER">
<TH>Toon</TH> <TH>Download</TH> <TH>Archive</TH>
</TR>
 <TR VALIGN="TOP" ALIGN="CENTER">
<TD>Dilbert</TD> <TD>no</TD> <TD>yes</TD>
</TR>
<TR VALIGN="TOP" ALIGN="CENTER">
<TD>Foxtrot</TD> <TD>no</TD> <TD>no</TD>
</TR>
<TR VALIGN="TOP" ALIGN="CENTER">
<TD>Grand Avenue</TD> <TD>yes</TD> <TD> yes</TD>
</TR>
</TABLE>
```

The script on the CD uses these features to provide a restricted directory-browsing service through a Web site. Just adjust the base directory specification for the download directory you want to use.

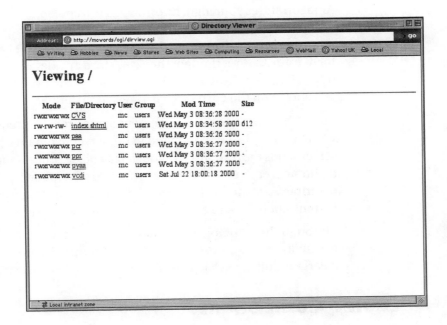

18 Setting Up a Cookie

CGI::Cookie
Lincoln Stein
www.perl.com

Unfortunately, Perl can't make chocolate-chip cookies for you, but it can make the sort of cookies used to store small pieces of site information within a browser. Cookies store Web-site login or greeting information, and even simple preferences. Your browser will only return the cookie to the host or domain configured by the cookie when created. Cookies are thus more secure than some people realize. Despite what you may have heard, it's impossible for a cookie to be obtained by anything other than the site that asks for it.

Amazon stores your login information in a cookie, so that it knows who you are; you may have noticed that whenever you visit the site it greets you by name and even customizes the layout. Cookies don't have to be related to login information, though; they can store any data you like. The Ananova news site (part of the Press Association) records your TV region so that it can show you the correct TV listings, for example.

The exchange of cookie data happens at the browser's request—for example, when it sends the GET command to the server to obtain a page and when the server sends the response. Although the cookie process sounds like a security nightmare, each cookie is tagged with and sent to specific hostnames, pages, or scripts. As standard, the cookie information is not encrypted, so you'll need to think about how to encrypt the data if it's sensitive.

Although the principles of the cookie are simple, setting up and using it manually can be quite complex. It won't surprise you to know, though, that a Perl module makes it all easier. That module is CGI::Cookie.

Cookie Components

Cookies consist of six pieces of information: the cookie name, value, expiry date, domain, path, and a simple security field.

The cookie name, of course, identifies the cookie. A server or domain can supply multiple cookies—you might want to store login and preference information separately, for example—so the name acts as a unique identifier.

The value is the information you want to store. Don't store too much information, as limited storage for cookies is available. You can supply a simple string, an array, or a hash reference. You can leave the formatting of the information to the CGI::Cookie module, but I'll look at that later.

Be careful when storing data in a cookie; although cookies are relatively secure, they are still open to abuse. Many browsers allow users to see the cookies stored there, and a Perl module will even allow you to access the information.

As a general rule, don't store passwords without some form of encryption. Unless absolutely vital, don't record the login and password within the same cookie; two cookies make it more difficult to collate the two pieces of information. If you want to use cookies for authentication purposes, consider using a system that separates the login authentication (see number 20 for information).

The browser uses the expiry date to identify when the stored cookie should be destroyed. If the date is set in the future, the browser will keep the cookie until the specified date. If the cookie is set in the past, then the browser will immediately dispose of the cookie. Setting a value of zero will cause the cookie only to be retained until the browser quits, so the cookie is never actually written to the hard disk.

The expiry information can be specified either explicitly or relatively. For example, you might want to create a cookie for a user's login process that expires in three months' time. You don't need to manually calculate the value; a relative expiry date is calculated from the time the cookie is generated. You can see a list of the supported date formats in the table.

Expiry	Description
+10y	Expires in ten years.
+3M	Expires in three months.
+1h	Expires one hour in the future.
+10m	Expires ten minutes in the future.
+30s	Expires 30 seconds from the time of creation.
Now	Expires when the user's browser quits.
Thursday, 25-Apr-1999 00:40:33 GMT	Expires at the specified date and time.
-1d	Expires immediately.

The domain is the partial or complete domain name for which the cookie is valid. The browser uses the domain field to determine where to send the cookie. The value of the domain can be a specific machine, such as www.mcwords.com, or a partial domain, such as .mcwords.com. The latter is useful for installations where multiple servers return information but need to provide authorization across all of them. Note that domains must contain at least two periods.

The path is a further classification for the browser to use when determining when the cookie should be sent to the server. If left unspecified, the cookie data will be sent with any page request. However, it's normal to specify the path to your CGI scripts directory. For example, if set to /cgi-bin, the cookie data will only be sent with requests for files within the /cgi-bin directory.

The final field is the security flag. If set to "1," the cookie will only be sent when sending requests over a secure communications channel, such as https. If left unset, the cookie will be sent with all requests, assuming the cookie matches the domain and path information.

Creating Cookies with CGI::Cookie

The CGI::Cookie module provides a number of different techniques for creating cookies. The primary method is to create a new cookie object and then use the header function from the CGI module to return the cookie data to the browser. The following code is an example:

```
$cookie = new CGI::Cookie(-name  => 'greeting',
                          -value => 'Martin'
                          );
print header(-cookie => $cookie);
```

But because a cookie tends to be used in combination with a form or other interactive solution, the cookie can be more easily integrated into the CGI system; then the CGI object can parse and return the cookie information, as shown:

```
my %cookie = (
                  -name => 'idksample',
                  -value => $login,
                  -path => '/',
                  -domain => 'mcwords.mchome.com',
                  -expires => '+1y',
                  );
my $query=new CGI;
print "Date: ", CGI::expires(0, 'http'), "\n";
print "Set-Cookie: ", $query->cookie(%cookie)) , "\n";
print "Content-type: text/html\n\n";
```

The sample script uses the foregoing method to identify and remember a user's form information before recording it into a cookie.

19 Reading a Cookie

CGI::Cookie
Lincoln Stein
www.perl.com

Once you've set a cookie, you need to be able to get the information back. It's actually provided by the browser during the request for the required URL.

The information is normally exported automatically by the Web server into the HTTP_COOKIE environment variable in the same format as a CGI request, with individual fields and values separated by equal signs and encoded using the same escaping sequence.

Parsing the information yourself is a time-consuming and, frankly, pointless process, especially when the CGI::Cookie module will do all the work for you.

The primary function for parsing the information is fetch, which returns a hash of all of the cookies sent by the browser to the Web server. Each key of the hash is the name of a cookie, so you can access multiple cookies by name:

```
my %cookies = fetch CGI::Cookie;
my $idkcookie = $cookies{'idksample'};
```

Once you have the cookie object, you can then use the various cookie methods to access the individual components. See the table for a list of the supported methods and the information returned. Note that these are generic methods—if called without any arguments, they return the cookie data; if supplied with arguments, they update the cookie object.

Method	Description
name	Get or set the cookie's name.
value	Get or set the cookie's value. If called in a scalar context, it will return only the first value of a multivalue cookie. If called in list context, it returns the cookie values as an array. If you supplied an array or hash as the value when creating the cookie, you can use the list returned to extract the data back into an array or hash value.

Method	Description
domain	**Get or set the cookie's domain.**
path	**Get or set the cookie's path.**
expires	**Get or set the cookie's expiry time. Note that the method returns the date and time string for the cookie, not the relative value.**

Once you've extracted the cookie object, you can then extract the cookie data—normally the only aspect you are really interested in. For a simple string, you can do so by coding the following:

```
$login = $idkcookie->value();
```

Or for a hash, you would code it as follows:

```
%user = $idkcookie->value();
```

Remember that if you are using the cookie as an authentication method, you should update the expiration time so the cookie doesn't unexpectedly expire. You can do so simply:

```
$idkcookie->expires("+1y");
```

Then remember to supply updated time back to the browser, so the cookie is updated for the next request:

```
print "Set-Cookie: $idkcookie\n";
print "Content-Type: text/html\n\n";
```

20 Using Sessions to Track a User

Session
Martin C. Brown
www.perl.com

It's no secret that many sites use Perl to handle most of their interactivity, but it's not always obvious how they achieve their tricks. When you visit e-commerce sites, such as Amazon, Outpost.com, or indeed any site that requires some sort of login, you'll probably wonder how they remember who you are as you click through the site.

Cookies, which we saw in the last two numbers, are a good solution and are used by most sites that offer an immediate greeting when you visit the home page. The problem with cookies is that they are relatively public and assume the user is willing to accept the cookie information in the first place. Much fuss has been made over cookie security. In principle, you shouldn't be able to access a cookie from a user's browser unless the cookie was registered against the domain of the server on which you were running. See the cookie examples in numbers 18 and 19 for further information.

So if a user has disabled cookies, how do you ensure security and provide the means to identify and track the user as he or she clicks through your site? In essence, it depends on what you are trying to achieve. If all you want is a way of validating a user to provide them access to a secure area that provides static HTML pages, then it's easier to use the security features of the Web server software than to produce something within Perl that does the same job.

In fact, you can even use CGI scripts within a secure area. Within Apache, set up your .htaccess file as normal and make sure the CGI directory where your scripts lie is within the confines of a secure directory. When you access a file in the directory for the first time, you'll be prompted for a login and password.

Within the script itself, you can access both the authorization type and the authorized user name by using the AUTH_TYPE and REMOTE_USER environment variables respectively. The variables enable you to track and identify a user within your scripts. Tracking what the user views while logged in is certainly possible: the standard Web log includes the user information if he or she has successfully logged in as the third field (see number 4).

But problems exist. You're relying on external influences to control and monitor your connection. You're also relying on an external security and authorization system over which you essentially have little control. There's not a facility for attaching additional information to use a login/password combination. When interfacing to a database that contains more than just simple user-identification information, you need a more advanced solution.

The Session Principle

A session ID is just a unique number that allows you to identify a user for a particular session. Generally, the way a session ID works is that the user logs in to the system and gets authorized. The process can be through the Web server security or through a user database; it's entirely up to you and the Perl script. Generally, it works in conjunction with a database so that other information about the user can also be tracked; for example, the user's name and address.

Once the authorization is approved, the user is given a session ID to identify him or her for the duration of the session. Each time the user views a page, the session ID is checked against a session database, which in turn gives you any user information you need.

An additional benefit of the session ID is that it is "public," so you are not distributing the user's login and/or password for each page view. In essence, the session ID is logically separate from the user's ID, with only the server being able to determine the link between the number and the authorization information.

Furthermore, because the session ID is used only for a single session, it will eventually expire. So even if the session information is stolen or identified by somebody, it'll be useless if the session is not used within a given time frame. Finally, because the session ID is never actually stored by the client (except in the user's history, but remember, it expires!), the user doesn't have to worry about security.

Of course, session IDs are not complete solutions to the problem of securely transferring data, but they do make a simple user-driven site more secure than constantly supplying the user's login as part of the request with each Web-page access.

In order for a session ID to work, you need to address a few issues:

◆ The session ID must be unique in order for it to be useful; you can't have two people with potentially the same ID.

◆ You need to store the session ID and any associated information; remember that the session ID is dynamic and therefore will be different each time a user logs in and visits the site. (But you still need to know who the user is!)

◆ You need to be able to expire the session ID and update the expiration information while the user is viewing the site.

◆ You need to be able to communicate and transfer the session ID between page selections.

◆ You also need to ensure that the session ID is not sequential or easily guessed.

Finally, the most important difference between the normal authorization systems and a session ID is that the site will need to be dynamically generated. This probably won't be an issue for a site that requires a login, but it's a consideration you need to include in the final equation.

Session ID Numbers

Creating a unique ID number is actually quite difficult. We can use random numbers, but they have a limited, unique scope, and it's not unknown (but not common either) for two random numbers picked within a few seconds of each other to be identical. Using a string of random numbers improves the chances, but there is still the possibility of the two strings being identical, especially on a busy site.

Using time information is also a bad idea, since it's possible, if not highly likely, for two requests to come in at the same time. Remember that we're dealing with a Web site, and if it's a busy site, you could have people from all over the world requesting a unique ID at the same time.

A second problem may not appear to be particularly obvious but is important just the same. That is, you need to ensure that the ID cannot be easily guessed or tried; the session ID could provide access to a site or the user's credit-card details. An ID purely based on a time and date can be easily guessed.

NOTE   You should never store credit-card or e-mail information in a cookie or session ID; store it in the database and then refer to it internally.

The solution is to use the time *and* random-number information to produce the ID string. If you use a fixed format and mix the random numbers in between the hours and other data, then you should have a random number that's unique enough for even the busiest site. In the module on the CD, the session ID is generated by extracting the date and time and mixing it with three different random numbers, as follows:

```
my $sessionid
    = sprintf("%02d%04d%02d-%02d%02d%04d-%d%d%d",
              $sec,pop @rand,$hour,$month,$min,
              pop @rand,pop @rand,$mday,$year);
```

The random numbers are first placed into a short array by calling Rand three times in quick succession. The result is an ID that will look something like 50649016-04016739-428025100.

I've done some tests to check how unique the ID was—I'd verified up to a million without coming across the same ID once! The time taken to generate each ID is negligible—I generated a million IDs within a few minutes on a fairly modest machine.

Storing Session IDs

As part of the process of isolating the user's information from the public accessibility of the Web, you need to ensure that the session ID is stored on the server with the user's authentication information and other information that you need ready access to when the session ID is validated.

For the sample script, I'm storing the information within a mySQL database, accessed through the DBI toolkit. The session database contains the session ID, the user and group details, a type (so you can identify the type of information the user can see), and an expiration time.

When a page is displayed, the session ID is checked against the database, first to identify a valid ID and then to check that the session hasn't expired. Once that's been verified, the function returns the user and group information to the calling script.

Session Expiration

To help ensure security, you must "expire" the ID. Expiration helps to ensure the uniqueness, because the user won't carry the same ID all the time. It also improves security by reducing the chances of the ID being used by somebody other than the genuine user; by the time the cracker has time to try the ID, the session will have expired and the user will need a login and password to get a new one.

NOTE   If you're unfamiliar with the term "cracker," it's the proper term for a malicious user. A hacker is just someone who plays with computers (I'm one!), but a cracker tries to crack into another machine and steal, modify, or destroy information.

You thus have a slight dilemma—you need to set a time long enough that a genuine user could take a short break or interruption without it expiring, but short enough that it can't be easily intercepted and misused. You can alleviate the first problem by updating the expiry time each time the session ID is verified; while in use, it's always fresh, but when it lapses it expires.

For a heavily interactive site such as one used for shopping, you can probably use an interval as low as 30 minutes, perhaps even 15. For a less security-conscious site, you can probably use a time as long as two hours.

Remember that although the session ID tracks against a user, it doesn't hold password information. Even if users try to view secure data, you still control how much information to provide them with—if you need to ask for the password again, you can without publicly exposing the login and password information.

Supplying Session Data

The final trick is the one that really makes it all work: you need to insert some code into the top of the script or scripts used to present your site. All you need to do is check for an incoming data field that will contain the session ID—I've used a field called `session` in the sample scripts. If it exists, use it in combination with the `check_session_id` function to verify the session with the session database. If no session is supplied, you can assume it's either invalid or has expired, and you provide the user with a login page to reconnect.

When supplying the session field, you can use some tricks to ensure that the information is exchanged correctly. For most simple instances, you can simply embed the field into a form like so:

```
<input type=hidden name=session value=sessionid>
```

Or you can append it to the end of a URL:

```
http://www.mchome.com/cgi/index.cgi?session=50649016-04016739-
428025100
```

To append the information, or indeed any information, to an existing URL, avoid parsing all supplied fields and formulating a new one; instead, just modify the one used to access script currently executing. The URL supplied to the Web server is available in the REQUEST_URI environment variable (or PATH_INFO on a Windows server). You can also try using the path_info method from the CGI module. The following code ensures that even if more information in the URL is supplied, it will still be included:

```
my $url = $ENV{REQUEST_URI};
$url .= "&session=50649016-04016739-428025100";
```

Furthermore, it also makes your script easily transferable to another machine. If the host on which the script is running changes, it doesn't matter because you're using the URL that was used to request the page in the first place!

Static Pages and Session IDs

It should be clear by now that the session system only works when you can safely exchange the ID between page impressions. So you can't use static pages, because there's no way of transferring the data between the static pages; instead, you have to use dynamically driven sites.

You can use static pages with a cookie, the one tool I'm avoiding here. Because the cookie information is stored with the browser and sent with each request to the server, the cookie information is still valid across any page, static or otherwise. You can also use sessions in combination with a cookie. All you do is use a cookie to store the session ID and then use that session ID embedded in the cookie to validate the user.

See numbers 18 and 19 for examples of how to use cookies within your scripts.

21 Sending Binary Files

Martin C. Brown
www.mcwords.com

You've already had a look at one solution that uses the techniques I'll be employing in this number (see number 2), but the same basic premise can be used in other arenas, too. The ability to download files has been around for a long time, but as the world of e-commerce, and more specifically downloadable software, increases, tools such as the following will become more popular.

Sending a binary file from Perl as part of a CGI script actually has little or nothing to do with Perl but is related to the HTTP headers sent back from a Perl script to the user's browser. Usually, you'll add something like the following line of code to return HTML data:

```
print "Content-type: text/html\n\n";
```

The content-type response just tells the browser (and the Web server) the type of file you are returning. The specification is in the form of a MIME (Multipurpose Internet Mail Extension) string. MIME is a set of standards used on the Internet to identify file names, file types, and the encoding format used when attaching files to e-mail messages.

Of special interest here is one MIME type, a slash-separated string that defines the base format type and subtype for a given file. A browser uses the MIME type (and if necessary the files extension) to decide how to handle the file when received. For example, the text/html indicates that a text file with embedded HTML codes is being transmitted. The browser will display the file as a standard HTML page.

Other formats, such as application/zip, are application specific, and zip indicates the file has been compressed using PKZip or a similar compression program. The browser will probably be configured to save the file to disk and might also call PKZip or Stuffit Expander to automatically expand and extract the files.

Some other examples of MIME types, taken from the mime.types file supplied with Apache, are shown as follows:

```
application/x-director      dcr dir dxr
application/x-dvi           dvi
application/x-gtar          gtar
application/x-gzip
application/x-javascript    js
application/x-sh            sh
application/x-shar          shar
```

application/x-shockwave-flash	swf
application/x-stuffit	sit
application/xml	
application/zip	zip
audio/32kadpcm	
audio/basic	au snd
audio/midi	mid midi kar
audio/mpeg	mpga mp2 mp3
audio/x-aiff	aif aiff aifc
audio/x-pn-realaudio	ram rm
audio/x-pn-realaudio-plugin	rpm
audio/x-realaudio	ra
audio/x-wav	wav
chemical/x-pdb	pdb xyz
image/gif	gif
image/jpeg	jpeg jpg jpe
image/png	png
image/tiff	tiff tif
message/http	
message/news	
message/partial	
message/rfc822	
text/html	html htm
text/plain	asc txt
text/rtf	rtf
text/sgml	sgml sgm
text/xml	xml
video/mpeg	mpeg mpg mpe
video/quicktime	qt mov

Note the file-extension column. It is used by Apache to automatically determine the format and send back a suitable HTTP header when a file is requested. Apache and other Web servers do such automatically for all files downloaded through a standard URL.

The base format is also significant. A text-based MIME type implies that the information may have different line termination and can be converted on the fly to the local format before being used. For HTML it won't make much difference, but for a text file, the line termination is important. Base formats like application and image are treated as binary streams and therefore not translated before use.

The script on the CD is for use on sites when you want the user to download a file without giving him or her direct access to it through the Web server. To use the script, copy it to your server and then supply the script with the location of the file you want to download. For example, you could code the following:

```
http://mysite.com/cgi-bin/download.pl?filename=myzip.zip
```

Note that the file will be downloaded from the $basedir directory. The location is set to the current directory in the base script; you'll need to change it to the location of the files you want to download.

The MIME types are embedded in the script to save you from loading an external file and key on the file extension. If the extension is not defined, it's transferred using the special application/octet-stream code, which basically means it's sent as an eight-bit binary file. It's up to the recipients' browser to decide how to handle the file.

The more important part is the send_file function. It takes two arguments, the file location and the MIME type to send to the user. If you need to perform any sort of authorization or other checks, place the information before the calls to send_file.

22 Cooperating with Apache

```
mod_perl
```
Doug MacEachern
```
perl.apache.org
```

Whenever you run a CGI script that uses Perl through your Web server, two factors slow down the execution:

1. The Web server must first start a new copy of the Perl interpreter.

2. The Perl interpreter must parse and recompile the script before executing it.

Although these two stages take only a few hundredths of a second when it is quiet, when the machine is under a heavy load the time taken can extend to seconds. Memory requirements also increase—running 10 instances of Perl simultaneously is vastly different than only using one.

The obvious solution for the first problem is to embed a Perl interpreter into the Web server, and then just start new threads to handle each query. The solution to the second problem is to store a ready-compiled version of the CGI script in memory, along with the interpreter, and then execute the script directly, instead of referring to the source script each time.

The solution to both problems is offered on a number of systems, most notably PerlEx, an extension available for the ActivePerl distribution that works with Microsoft's Internet Information Server, and mod_perl, an extra module that can be built into the Apache executable. Both offer the same basic facilities: they allow you to execute Perl scripts without using an external interpreter and without having to recompile the source each time. The speed increase you gain using either of these systems is entirely subject to your script; increases of 100 to 2,000 percent are sometimes quoted!

Other advantages exist beyond the obvious speed increases. First and foremost, because mod_perl embeds Perl right into the Apache server, it's possible to get Perl to access Apache configuration information and even to provide extensive internal information on the Apache Web server, which can be useful when monitoring performance.

The Perl/Apache advantage works in the other direction, too—Apache can use aspects of the Perl interpreter to provide even more functionality. For example, you use Perl in combination with the DBI module and a SQL database to provide Apache authentication services instead of the normal text or DBM file-based systems. You'll see an example in the next number when I look at Apache authorization.

Configuring Apache

To get the mod_perl module to start executing your scripts, you need to modify the httpd.conf file so that Apache knows when to use mod_perl rather than starting an external process. There are two ways to do so. The first is to introduce a Location directive, either in the main file or within a VirtualHost directive. The directive should point to the directory that will hold the Perl scripts you want executed by mod_perl. The following is an example:

```
Alias /mod_perl/  /usr/local/http/htdocs/mod_perl
<Location /mod_perl>
```

```
SetHandler  perl-script
PerlHandler Apache::Registry
Options +ExecCGI
</Location>
```

You can also place the SetHandler, PerlHandler, and Options tags into the .htaccess file for a specific directory.

Alternatively (and this is my preferred method), you could place a Files directive into the configuration file:

```
<Files ~ "\.plx$">
        SetHandler  perl-script
        PerlHandler Apache::Registry
        Options ExecCGI
</Files>
```

In this case all files with a .plx extension will be executed through mod_perl. Other scripts can thus more easily run as normal, or mod_perl and standard CGI scripts can run alongside each other within the same directory.

How mod_perl Works

The mod_perl extension is not like a typical Perl module. Unlike the other modules you've seen here, it doesn't merge Perl with an external C module; instead, it merges Apache with the Perl libraries.

Therefore, the Apache server has direct access to the interpreter used to run Perl scripts normally. The first time a script is run, it's compiled into the internal bytecode used by Perl and then stored. The bytecode is executed each time the script is called and when a new thread is started using the built-in interpreter. The stored bytecode eliminates the need either to start a whole new process or to parse the script each time.

Because the scripts are not run within the relative safety of an external interpreter, you need to be careful of the following:

◆ Beware of variables that could get overfilled with data. Because the script execution is permanent, you could fill up more and more RAM with useless variables.

◆ Be wary of scripts that talk to the modules relying on C libraries. A failure in one of these libraries could have a damaging effect on your Web server.

◆ Make sure your script checks all executions of external programs. It's possible to run multiple instances of the same program; they will hang around the system and slow it down.

◆ Make sure that in your script the locking mechanisms that allow you to access multiple resources work effectively.

Converting Scripts for mod_perl

Provided you use the CGI module, there isn't much you should need to do in order to convert the script for use under the mod_perl Apache module. In fact, you can reduce the changes for any script to a minimum:

◆ Use CGI for all parsing of input values.

◆ Use CGI to emit headers—the simplest form is:

```
my $query = new CGI;
print $query->header('text/html');
```

◆ Switch on warnings. The first time the script is run by mod_perl, any command-line switches will be honored.

◆ Use the strict pragma.

◆ Use the Perl taint mode by supplying the -T command-line option.

That should be it. Keep to those basic rules and you shouldn't have to perform any other type of conversion on your CGI scripts to get them to work OK. More importantly, the scripts will continue to work as normal CGI scripts without modification.

23 Using Apache Authentication

HTTPD::UserAdmin
Doug MacEachern
www.cpan.org

I've already looked at some methods for authenticating and tracking users. The module discussed here provides some generic methods for managing the authentication databases used by Apache.

The HTTPD::UserAdmin module supports the creation and management of authentication databases. You can use the module to control and create the Web users for authentication in Apache entirely from within the confines of a Perl script. You can use this module to create a new user for a directory secured through the standard Apache security mechanisms, without the need for either cookies or sessions to track the progress of a user through your site. You still need a session- or cookie-based system to support an e-commerce site, but for simple authentication the system will work fine.

Using HTTPD::UserAdmin

The module supports a management interface to three basic authentication systems. The file is just a standard text file, much like the Unix /etc/passwd file that contains user names and their passwords encrypted using the standard crypt() function. A DBM (database management) database stores the data into a DBM file. The database file is much more practical for very large login databases than simply using a text file—a text-based system would require Apache to load and search the entire text file each time the user logs in to the site, which is not particularly efficient.

The last format, DBI, allows the module to manage a user-authentication system stored within a DBI-compliant database (for example, MySQL and PostgreSQL). You can use DBI for more complex sites, or for systems that need a login that integrates with a larger database system. Any database that works with DBI will work with this module, but only the mod_perl extension, discussed in the previous number, will actually support authentication. Apache supports Text and DBM authentication natively.

The module works through an object interface, so the first task is to create a new HTTPD::UserAdmin object:

```
my $useradmin = new HTTPD::UserAdmin(DBType => 'Text',
                                     DB => '.htpasswd',
                                     Server => 'ncsa');
```

The new method accepts a list of arguments that are interpreted as a hash to configure the system. All authentication systems support a set of generic arguments. In the foregoing example, I simply created a link to a text-file-based authentication system. The equivalent for opening a DBM database would be:

```
my $useradmin = new HTTPD::UserAdmin(DBType => 'DBM',
                                     DB => '.htpasswd',
                                     Server => 'ncsa');
```

Other arguments are specific to the DBM or DBI authentication methods. You can see a full list of the configuration options in the table.

Option	Level	Description
DBType	Generic	The type of database, either "DBM," "Text," or "SQL" (default is "DBM").
DB	Generic	The database name (default is ".htpasswd" for DBM and Text databases).
Server	Generic	HTTP server name (default is the generic class that works with NCSA, Apache, and possibly others).
Encrypt	Generic	Either "crypt," "MD5," or "none."
Locking	Generic	Boolean; for locking Text and DBM files. (Default is "true.")
Path	Generic	Relative DB files are resolved to this value (Default is ".")
Debug	Generic	Boolean; turns on debug mode.
Flags	Generic	The read, write, and create flags. Flags are defined as a string, using the first letter of read, write, and create. Supported combinations are "rwc," "rw," "r," and "w."
DBMF	DBM	The DBM file implementation to use. (Default is "NDBM.")
Mode	DBM	The file-creation mode; defaults to "0644."
Host	DBI	Server hostname.

Option	Level	Description
Port	**DBI**	**Server port.**
User	**DBI**	**Database login name.**
Auth	**DBI**	**Database login password.**
Driver	**DBI**	**Driver for DBI. (Default is "mSQL.")**
UserTable	**DBI**	**Table with field names below.**
NameField	**DBI**	**Field for the name. (Default is "user.")**
PasswordField	**DBI**	**Field for the password. (Default is "password.")**

For text and DBM databases, if the database file specified does not already exist, a new file is created. For DBI databases the methods are slightly different—additions, updates, and deletions are handled using SQL, so you need to define to the system the database, table, and field names to be used for authentication, as shown:

```
@ my $useradmin =
    new HTTPD::UserAdmin(DBType =>          "SQL",
                         Host =>            "",
                         Port =>            "",
                         DB =>              "www",
                         User =>            "",
                         Auth =>            "",
                         Encrypt =>         "crypt",
                         Driver =>          "mSQL",
                         Server =>          "apache",
                         UserTable =>       "www-users",
                         NameField =>       "user",
                         PasswordField =>   "password",
                        );
```

Once the object has been successfully created, you then just need to call different methods to create, delete, and update individual users. To add a new user, code something like the following:

```
$useradmin->add('mc','password');
```

To delete a user, insert a line similar to the following:

```
$useradmin->delete('user');
```

To change the password for an existing user, use the following format:

```
$useradmin->update('mc','password');
```

The script included on the CD is a very simple CGI script that allows you to create and edit users in a text file.

Configuring Apache

You control the access of your directories through Apache in two stages. The first is that you must have configured the directory structure within the main `httpd.conf` file to ensure that an `.htaccess` file can override the directory permissions and accesses. To do so, add a `<Directory>` directive to the configuration file, as shown:

```
<Directory /usr/local/http/webs/test/secure>
    AllowOverrides All
</Directory>
```

The second stage is to create the necessary `.htaccess` file that points to the authorization database. A simple `.htaccess` file follows:

```
AuthType Basic
AuthUserFile /usr/local/http/webs/test/cgi-bin/.htpasswd
AuthName "Members Area"
require valid-user
```

The `AuthType` defines the authorization system being used. You should probably use "Basic." The `AuthUserFile` is the name of the text file to use when searching for a matching login name. If you want to use a DBM file, you need to use the `AuthUserDBMFile` instead. There are also corresponding entries for an `AuthGroupFile` and `AuthGroupDBMFile` to hold group details. You'll need to use one of the authorization extensions for Apache if you want to use a SQL server—visit www.apache.org.

The `AuthName` is the name of the secure site to be highlighted in login dialogue to the user. Finally, the `require` statement defines under what circumstances an "authorized" connection should be validated. In this case you require a valid user (i.e., a matching user/password combination).

You can restrict the settings for a current directory to a select set of users with the user option; for example, consider the following:

```
require user mc admin
```

The code would only accept a valid login in by either mc or admin–even if other logins were valid and verified against the password databases. As an extension of that, the subsequent directive would only allow users who are members of the admin group access to the directory:

```
require group admin
```

....

N O T E   The companion HTTPD::GroupAdmin module is needed for group file administration within Perl.

The prior code is useful for supporting restricted access to a directory tree, and then subdividing access to specific directories within that tree. For example, you might require a valid password for access to the entire directory tree, but only allow certain users into an administration directory that contains administration scripts. By using the password file, the user will only have to enter the login/password combination once to access all the directories of which he or she is a member.

24   FAQ Management

FAQ::OMatic
Jon Howell
www.dartmouth.edu/cgi-bin/cgiwrap/jonh/faq.pl

The phenomenon of the FAQ, the Frequently Asked Questions, document is almost as meteoric as that of the Internet. FAQ documents are now quite commonplace, not only on Web sites, but also in paper documents, leaflets, and even some magazines.

The principle of the FAQ is very simple; a series of questions and corresponding answers, perhaps ordered into individual sections, focus on a topic. Each question, and each section, is generally given a number. For example, you could have a question numbered 2.13—the 13th question in the second section.

A Web-site FAQ is normally produced using a single document that contains a list of questions at the top, which then links to the corresponding answer later in that same document. But managing an FAQ document can be a time-consuming task. If you introduce a new question into a section, the others need to renumbered.

It's also a good idea to track the changes you make to the document. You can use CVS (Concurrent Versioning System) or RCS (Revision Control System) for this task, but it's yet another stage in the production process. The complication gets worse if more than one person is responsible for updating the FAQ.

The obvious solution is to develop some form of overall structure using either a database or set of simple files that allows you to update the information without affecting the overall structure. For the interactivity and multiuser problems, it makes sense to use a CGI script to update it all. You can continue to use CVS or RCS to track problems.

Once again, it won't surprise you to know a solution already exists; in this case it's the FAQ::OMatic module. The module is entirely self-contained and provides everything you need to build up and later edit your FAQ.

To install the module, follow these steps:

1. Extract the module from its archive.

2. Change to the archive directory.

3. Run the following:

```
$ perl Makefile.PL
$ make
$ make install
```

You'll then get a message that includes an administration password; make a note of it and then copy the script fom to the CGI directory of your Web server. Then all you need to do is open up a browser and follow the on-screen prompts to define the parameters about your FAQ, such as where the files should be stored and how information should be displayed.

After configuration (which takes only five minutes and answering a few questions), all you need to do is populate your FAQ with sections, subsections, and the questions (actually called answers by the FAQ-O-Matic system).

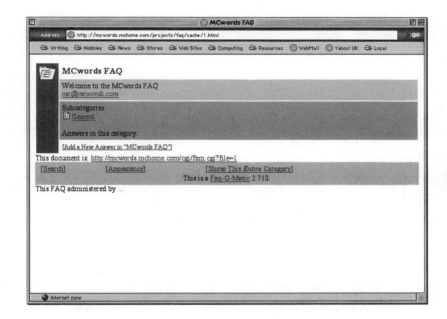

Networking

Networking is taken for granted now. Most companies have networks to support e-mail and share files and printers. Some people even have networks in their homes. But everyone can use a more flexible way of communicating over a network and talking to some of the network services.

25 Resolving DNS Information

```
Net::DNS
```
Michael Fuhr
`www.dimensional.com/~mfuhr/perldns/`

Every machine on a TCP/IP network, including those hooked into the Internet, must have its own unique address. When two machines communicate with each other a TCP/IP network, IP addresses identify each machine and also the destination of the packets that make up the communication channel between the two machines.

But humans are pretty terrible at remembering numbers. If I asked any reader of this book how many telephone numbers he or she could remember, then I imagine I could probably count them on my 20 digits (hands and feet!).

That's why Domain Name Service, or DNS, is so useful. It provides translation from the textual domain names to the IP addresses required for communication. A full description of the DNS system is far beyond the scope of this book, but a quick overview is always useful.

The DNS system works very simply. Collections of machines are allotted into domains—for example, `sybex.com`. Within the domain are a number of different pieces of information, ranging from a list of the authoritative domain servers— machines that hold authentic information about the domain—to the individual IP addresses for each machine.

When you look up an address, such as `www.sybex.com`, your machine talks to the domain-name server, either a local machine or one at your ISP, configured for your network. In most cases the sequence for converting the name to an address works as follows. First your domain server tries to determine the IP address by checking its own database, if it's a local address, or its cache, if it's an external address. If the address cannot be found, the server talks to one of its peering servers—that is, other servers that might know the information. If the address still can't be resolved, the server will contact one of the root domain servers that hold authoritative information about all the domains and the servers responsible for them.

Armed with the information about the correct machine to talk to, your domain server can then query the authoritative server directly to resolve the address. If it's still not found, the address probably doesn't exist.

The whole process works in milliseconds. With some exceptions you can generally obtain the address of any machine on the Internet in less than a second.

Perl provides two built-in functions, `gethostbyname` and `gethostbyaddr`, which in turn use the underlying operating system's functions to resolve names into addresses and vice versa. The functions are fairly limited and only resolve the information very simply.

Among the other pieces of information stored within domain records is the detail of the MX, or Mail Exchanger host. The MX data tells e-mail software what machine to send an e-mail to when given only a domain name. For example, to send an e-mail to me, you'd use `mc@whoever.com`. But no machine resolves from the `whoever.com` domain.

Instead, MX records on the DNS servers associated with the `whoever.com` domain point to the mail exchangers—the servers that accept mail for the `whoever.com` domain. If you have software capable of resolving that information for you, such as `nslookup`, you can see the information for the real servers as follows:

```
$ nslookup
Default Server:  twinspark.mchome.com
Address:  198.112.10.130

> set type=mx
> whoever.com
Server:  twinspark.mchome.com
Address:  198.112.10.130

whoever.com      preference = 20, mail exchanger = mail-intake-
   2.iname.net
```

```
whoever.com       preference = 30, mail exchanger = mail-intake-
   3.iname.net
whoever.com       preference = 10, mail exchanger = mail-intake-
   1.iname.net
whoever.com       nameserver = ns1.mail.com
whoever.com       nameserver = ns2.mail.com
mail-intake-2.iname.net internet address = 165.251.8.73
mail-intake-2.iname.net internet address = 165.251.8.33
...
mail-intake-2.iname.net internet address = 165.251.8.184
mail-intake-2.iname.net internet address = 165.251.8.194
ns1.mail.com      internet address = 165.251.1.2
ns2.mail.com      internet address = 165.251.1.3
```

Within Perl you can use the Net::DNS module from Michael Fuhr to extract all sorts of information from the DNS records. It can even be used to associate dynamically assigned IP addresses (like those issued by DHCP) to domain names using dynamic DNS.

DHCP—the system used on dial-up, cable, and DSL connections to share a pool of IP addresses—makes it difficult to host domains or other services, because the IP address is different each time the user connects. Dynamic DNS is an extension to the basic DNS system that gets around the problem by dynamically pointing a domain name to an IP address.

The Net::DNS Module

The main component of the Net::DNS system is the Net::DNS::Resolver module. It provides the base object class used for all queries. Each resolver object supports two methods—search and query. The search method allows you to simply ask the DNS system about an address. The answer will contain information about all the matching records for the given address.

The search method is identical to simply entering the domain name on the command line within nslookup. For example, to get all of the address records for a given name, you could code the following:

```
use Net::DNS;
$res = new Net::DNS::Resolver;
$query = $res->search($ARGV[0]);
if ($query)
```

```
    {
        foreach $rr ($query->answer)
        {
            print $rr->address, "\n" if ($rr->type eq "A");
        }
    }
    else
    {
        die "Can't find $ARGV[0]: ", $res->errorstring, "\n";
    }
```

The method returns an array of resource record (RR) objects, which contain the individual information for each name/IP-address combination. The information returned is more than what is normally returned from an information request. You can see a list of the methods and the information they return in the table.

Method	Description
address	Returns the IP address in the form "x.x.x.x."
print	Prints the record to the standard output using the string method for the RR record.
string	Returns a string version of the RR information.
rdatastr	Returns a string containing RR-specific information.
name	Returns the name of the domain to which the record belongs.
type	Returns a string defining the record's type.
class	Returns the record's class.
ttl	Returns the record's time-to-live information.
rdlength	Returns the length, in bytes, of the record data.
rdata	Returns the raw record data in binary format.

The RR object is a generic object. Specific objects also exist for the different entry types. See the module documentation for more information.

Preventing Spam

Stopping spam may not seem like an obvious usage of the `Net::DNS` module, but you can use the module to help test for one of the major reasons spam exists. Spam, or Unsolicited Bulk Email (UBE), is the scourge of the Internet. I get three or four messages a day offering me get-rich-quick schemes, offshore-investment opportunities, or worse.

Spam is despised so much that numerous sites and services try to reduce or eliminate it at its source. Most spam is sent through an open SMTP server—a mail server that doesn't monitor who the sender and recipient are. Thus, anybody with an e-mail program and a list of e-mail addresses can start sending e-mail unchecked. Systems administrators can get around the obstacle by only allowing users to send and receive e-mail with people in the domains they manage.

Checking whether a server allows spam to be sent is relatively simple; you can just set up your mail program to send to the offending server and try sending a message. If it gets through (and you're not an approved sender or recipient), the server probably has a problem.

The script included on the CD does all the work for you. It uses the `Net::DNS` module to find all of the SMTP servers for a domain, and then uses the `Net::SMTP` module to send the message. By monitoring the return values for each SMTP command, you can determine whether the server is open or secure.

To use, just supply the name of the domain or a machine within the domain. Consider the following:

```
$ cksmtp.pl mchome.com
Checking mail forwarding for mchome.com
Checking mail.mchome.com
mail.mchome.com seems to allow anonymous sending
```

Because you're using the `Net::DNS` module, you check all the machines defined within the domain as MX hosts, like so:

```
$ ./cksmtp.pl demon.net
Checking mail forwarding for demon.net
Checking internal.mail.demon.net
Safe
Checking relay-1.mail.demon.net
Safe
```

```
Checking relay-2.mail.demon.net
Safe
```

The method isn't foolproof, unfortunately, because some mail servers will accept mail and then dump it later. The script will warn about an unsafe site, even though the site may actually work to prevent spam. You'll need to monitor the e-mails (make sure you change the e-mail address to your own, please!) to determine whether the site is safe or not.

I've used this script in the past to quickly check the domain identified in the mail headers as sending the spam message. I've then contacted the postmaster to warn about the problem.

26 Getting E-mail from a POP Server

```
Net::POP3
Graham Barr
www.cpan.org
```

If you're like me, you probably have a number of different e-mail accounts that you use for a variety of reasons. I've got a personal e-mail address, a few business addresses, and a couple for different mailing lists and other discussion lists, not to mention the free ones on Yahoo!, Hotmail, and others.

Keeping track of them can be a nightmare. Even with modern e-mail applications like Outlook and Eudora, just collating and reading your e-mail can take hours.

Probably the most annoying aspect for me is that some accounts I just don't use regularly enough to warrant a daily check, and perhaps not even a weekly check. Worse still, these accounts are POP accounts that I can only access interactively. Because I already have a mail server in the office, I wrote a simple script that would collect the mail and forward it as normal SMTP mail to the local server. Using this tool, you can easily forward mail from a POP account to your main account without having to manually transfer the messages.

Using Net::POP3

Accessing any POP server is very easy—providing you know some basic commands. POP works on a simple request/response system, much like FTP and SMTP. You send a request to the server, and it returns the information to you and waits for your next request. A typical conversation would go something like:

Client: Login

Server: OK, password?

Client: Password

Server: OK, you have 2 messages

Client: List message IDs

Server: OK, message 1 is 540 bytes, message 2 is 1623 bytes

Client: Get message 1

Within POP3 the commands used are USER, PASS, LIST, and GET. The Net::POP3 module provides you with an object-based interface to a POP3 server; the supported methods match the basic commands supported by most POP3 servers. You can see a list of the supported commands in the table. Note that some may be unsupported on some machines.

Command	Description
user (*USER*)	**Login using** *USER*.
pass (*PASS*)	**Send the password** *PASS*. **Once authorized, returns the number of the messages in the mailbox, or** undef **if the login failed.**
login ([*USER* [, *PASS*]])	**Login using** *USER* **and** *PASS*. **If** *PASS* **is not given then the user's** .netrc **file is searched for a matching host/user combination. If** *USER* **is not supplied, the current login is used instead. Once authorized, returns the number of the messages in the mailbox, or** undef **if the login failed.**
apop (*USER*, *PASS*)	**Login using a secure transaction, rather than clear text. Requires the** MD5 **package.**

Command	Description
top (*MSGNUM* [, *NUMLINES*])	Gets up to *NUMLINES* lines starting from the header of the selected *MSGNUM*. Returns an array reference of the individual lines.
list ([*MSGNUM*])	Returns the size of *MSGNUM* in octets (bytes). If called without an argument, returns a hash containing the message numbers of the undeleted messages and their corresponding size.
get (*MSGNUM*)	Returns the lines of the message identified by *MSGNUM* from the server in the form of an array reference.
last ()	Returns the highest message number currently on the server.
popstat ()	Returns the number of undeleted messages and the size of the mailbox.
uidl ([*MSGNUM*])	Returns the unique identifier for the supplied *MSGNUM*, or if no message number is supplied, returns a hash containing the message numbers and the corresponding unique identifiers.
delete (*MSGNUM*)	Marks message *MSGNUM* to be deleted from the remote mailbox. Marked messages will be removed from the mailbox when the server connection is closed via quit.
reset ()	Resets the status of the connection to the POP3 server. Resets the list of messages marked for deletion so that all messages marked within the current session are left undeleted.
quit ()	Quit and close the connection to the remote POP3 server. Any messages marked as deleted will be deleted from the remote mailbox.

Note that message numbers are not consistent across different sessions—that is, the message number is unique for each session.

To use the script, supply the POP server, login, password, and the address to which you want the e-mail resent, as the following example shows:

```
$ remail.pl pop mc password mc@mcwords.com
```

The code will download all the e-mail and resend it to the given address. Note that it does not, by default, delete the e-mail from the server. If you want to delete, uncomment the call to delete within the script.

27 Getting Usenet Messages

```
Net::NNTP
```
Graham Barr
```
www.cpan.org
```

Before the World Wide Web, one of the biggest uses of the Internet after e-mail was Usenet. Usenet is a bit like your local bar, only to a greater degree—hundreds of people talking about hundreds of different topics in hundreds of little groups and huddles.

But with so many newsgroups, it's difficult to keep track of what you are interested in, especially at a specific level. For example, you can browse the alt.fan.douglas-adams newsgroup, but if you only like his *Long Dark Tea Time of the Soul* book, you could waste much time reading messages not pertaining to the book.

As part of a solution to this problem, I wrote a script that would download all the messages from a Usenet news server into text files that I could later search for more information. Although it wastes a little bit of online time, it compresses the process into an allotted slot each day, and then I can read the messages whenever I like. I can even read messages posted two or three weeks ago, useful when you consider that most servers delete messages that are more than a week old.

NOTE If you want to search old news without using this script, check out dejanews.com.

How Usenet Works

Usenet works by taking a single news message and supplying it to a combination of clients and servers. For clients it enables them to read the messages, and for servers it provides a method for copying the message so it can be read by a different set of users. So, if I post a message to my ISP's server in the United Kingdom, the message will be distributed first to other ISPs in the United Kingdom, and then to others in Europe, the United States, and the rest of the world. It takes between a few hours and a few days for a single newsgroup message to be distributed to all the servers that support that newsgroup throughout the world, which makes Usenet a truly global discussion system.

Messages are divided into newsgroups—top-level descriptions of a particular set of messages. The Douglas Adams fan group is an example, as is the alt.music.tmbg group for fans of They Might Be Giants. Each message can be posted to multiple newsgroups. In addition each message can also include details on the distribution, which controls where the message is sent. A message posted to the uk.jobs group, for example, might have a distribution of "UK," so that only U.K. Usenet servers hold the message and distribute it to other servers.

Usenet messages are stored in different ways on different machines. Regardless of the storage mechanism, messages can be accessed in two different ways, by message ID and by message number. The message ID is a unique ID given to each message posted on Usenet. Message numbers are only unique within a given newsgroup.

The server on which the message is posted generates the message ID. For example, the message ID for a message created on the BT Internet news server might be:

```
B579902C96683BA83@host62-7-116-162.btinternet.com
```

The message ID is independent of the newsgroup in which the message was posted. So you can download any message by its message ID without having to worry about the current newsgroup.

The message number, distinguished from the message ID, is a unique number given to a message within a newsgroup. The number is unique only for the current session on the current server, because it's the number given to an article when it is received and stored on the server. Message numbers are therefore server and group specific, whereas a message ID is completely server and newsgroup neutral.

Understanding the difference is important; when reading Usenet news you can opt to download either a message by its ID or number. For the former, you can theoretically be anywhere, but the latter format requires that you change to a specific group before requesting the message.

The Net::NNTP Module

Like the Net::POP3 module, the Net::NNTP module provides an object-based interface that matches the commands supported by a NNTP server. To open a connection, just create a new Net::NNTP object supplying the name of the server, like so:

```
use Net::NNTP;

$nntp = Net::NNTP->new("news");
$nntp->quit;
```

Once open, you then use the methods outlined in the table to get a list of newsgroups, messages, or a single message.

Method	Description
article ([*MSGID*|*MSGNUM*], [*FH*])	**Returns the entire message, with the header and body separated by a blank line as an array reference—each array element holding a single line. The** *MSGID* **is the unique ID for the message, and** *MSGNUM* **is the message number within the current newsgroup. If** *FH* **is supplied, then it's taken as a valid filehandle, and the text is written to that file directly.**

Method	Description
body ([*MSGID*|*MSGNUM*], [*FH*])	**Returns the body only for a specific message ID or number. Information is written to the file referenced by** *FH*, **if supplied.**
head ([*MSGID*|*MSGNUM*], [*FH*])	**Returns the header only for a specific message ID or number. Information is written directly to the file referenced by** *FH*, **if supplied.**
nntpstat ([*MSGID*|*MSGNUM*])	**Sets the current article pointer within the current newsgroup to the message referred to by** *MSGNUM* **or to the message identified by the unique** *MSGID*. **Returns the message ID for the current article.**
group ([*GROUP*])	**If supplied with an argument, changes the currently selected newsgroup. If not supplied any arguments, returns the current newsgroup. In a scalar context only, the group is returned, whereas in an array context, the return value is a list containing the number of articles in the group, the first article number and last article number, and the group name.**
ihave (*MSGID* [, *MESSAGE*])	**Indicates to the server that the client has a given article ID. If the message has been supplied (as an array of message lines) as the second argument, the message text is sent to the server. It is useful for exchanging articles between two servers. This is how some servers exchange messages, by appearing as clients and telling the server which message it already has.**
last ()	**Moves the current article pointer to the last message within the current group.**
date ()	**Returns the date on the server in seconds since the epoch.**
postok ()	**Returns true if the server's initial response indicated that messages from the client can be posted.**

Method	Description
list ()	Returns a hash that contains a list of all of the newsgroups supported and stored by the server. The hash keys are the names of the groups, and the value is a reference to an array containing the first and last article numbers and any information flags. Be warned that the method can take a long time to complete.
newgroups (SINCE [, DISTRIBUTIONS])	Returns the newsgroup information as per list, but only for newsgroups newer than the given time SINCE (YYMMDDHHMM). The DISTRIBUTIONS is a distribution pattern or reference to an array of patterns against which the groups should be matched.
newnews (SINCE [, GROUPS [, DISTRIBUTIONS]])	Returns a reference to a list of message IDs posted after SINCE, in the matching GROUPS and DISTRIBUTIONS, if supplied.
next ()	Moves the current article pointer to the next article in the current newsgroup.
post ([MESSAGE])	Posts MESSAGE, which should be an array or reference to an array of message lines, to the server. The newsgroup and distribution information will be extracted from the message and an error will be raised if they are either unspecified or do not match the currently supported newsgroup list.
slave ()	Indicates to the remote server that the connection is not from a true client but another server. It does not affect the communications process but does help the server when initiating ihave methods.
quit ()	Closes the remote connection.

The sample script works very simply by creating a directory for a given newsgroup, into which you store the messages. The directory also contains a file that stores the message number so that you can be sure you don't download messages you already have. For example, to download the messages for the alt.fan.douglas-adams group, code the following:

```
$ nntpgrab.pl alt.fan.douglas-adams
```

28 Searching a Search Engine

WWW::Search
John Heidemann, Martin Thurn
www.cpan.org

Back in number 12 I looked at a technique for producing a searchable index for your own Web site so you could provide your users a way of searching the site for information. However, you may want to provide your users the ability to search the Web with search engines such as AltaVista or Yahoo!. But you probably don't want the information to be displayed as an AltaVista page; you want to add your own window dressing and information to the list of matches returned.

The WWW::Search module provides a simple interface for communicating directly with an Internet search engine and getting the responses. The current list of search engines and their support within the WWW::Search system can be seen in the table. You can see from the table that the supported-search-engine list is quite extensive, and future support is planned for some of the local search engines, such as Microsoft's Index Server.

Search Engine(Module)	Status
AltaVista	**Working**
AltaVista::AdvancedNews	**Not Working**
AltaVista::AdvancedWeb	**Not Working**
AltaVista::Careers	**Working**
AltaVista::Intranet	**Working**
AltaVista::News	**Not Working**
AltaVista::Web	**Working**
AOL	**Working (see NetFind)**

Search Engine(Module)	Status
AOL::Classifieds::Employment	**Working**
Crawler	**Partially Working**
Dice	**Working**
Excite::News	**Working**
ExciteForWebServers	**Not Working**
Fireball	**Working**
FolioViews	**Working**
Gopher	**Not Working**
HeadHunter	**Working**
HotFiles	**Working**
Infoseek	**Working**
Infoseek::Companies	**Working**
Infoseek::Email	**Not Working**
Infoseek::News	**Working**
Infoseek::Web	**Working**
Livelink	**Not Working**
LookSmart	**Working**
Lycos	**Working**
Lycos::Pages	**Defunct**
Lycos::Sites	**Defunct**
MetaCrawler	**Working**
Metapedia	**Working**
Monster	**Working**

Search Engine(Module)	Status
MSIndexServer	**Not Working**
NetFind	**Working**
NorthernLight	**Working**
Null	**Working**
PLweb	**Not Working**
Profusion	**Defunct**
Search97	**Not Working**
SFgate	**Working**
Simple	**Not Working**
Verity	**Not Working**
VoilaFr	**Working**
WebCrawler	**Working**
Yahoo::Classifieds::Employment	**Uncertain**

To use the module, just create a WWW::Search object, supplying the name of the engine you want to search, and then submit a search query to the engine. The following is an example:

```
my $search = new WWW::Search('AltaVista');
$search->native_query(WWW::Search::escape_query($query));
```

You can then iterate over the resulting matches or return the matches in big hash. The former is better, as it avoids creating huge internal structures. The object returned from each iteration contains the information for a given result, including its title, descriptive text, and the URL. You can use this information to provide your own list. To iterate over the site, use the next_result method like so:

```
while (my $result = $search->next_result())
{
}
```

For the script on the CD, I've written a simple AltaVista-search-engine interface as a CGI script that you could include on your own site. The graphic shows a sample of the output.

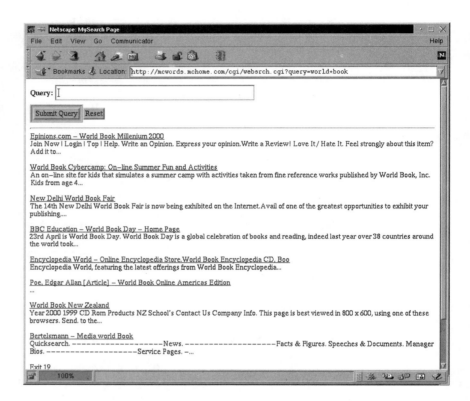

29 Running a Socket-Based Server

IO::Socket
Built-in
www.perl.com

You will sometimes not want to rely on a "standard" protocol such as NNTP or FTP for communication; instead, you may want your own custom socket-based server that can listen for and respond to requests directly.

I was in just such a situation many years ago. I needed an HTTP server to run on a special port number but couldn't rely on a program like Apache, because the server would be supplied as part of an installation program. That is, the Web server would provide help information for the user.

The solution was to use Perl to build a very cut-down Web server. All it needed to do was respond to simple GET requests from a browser—the type of requests that obtain the HTML and graphics files that make up a typical site.

Listening for Socket Connections

Perl provides a number of built-in socket functions that create a socket handle (which Perl can use as a normal filehandle) and then listen and accept new requests. The process of setting up a server is more complicated than opening a client socket. The server socket must be bound to a local address—the same IP address and port the clients will use to connect to the server. The socket must be set to a listen state where it sits and waits for new connections.

The process of setting up a server is as follows:

1. Create and open a local socket, specifying the protocol family (PF_INET or PF_UNIX), socket type, and top-level protocol number (TCP, UDP, etc.).

2. Determine the local service-port number on which you want to listen for new connections.

3. Set any options for the newly created socket.

4. Bind the socket to an IP address and service port on the local machine.

5. Set the socket to the listen state, specifying the size of the queue used to hold pending connections.

You can perform the preceding steps using the built-in functions, but it's very time-consuming to learn about them. Instead, you can use the

IO::Socket module to do all the work. You resolve the five steps into a single statement:

```perl
my $socket = IO::Socket::INET->new( LocalPort => 8008,
                                    Listen => 5,
                                    Reuse => 1 );
```

The result is a filehandle that you can use to accept new connections from clients. Filehandles and sockets are treated the same in Perl.

Accepting/Processing Connections

There are different ways of accepting connections (I'll look at one alternative in the next number), but it's normal to use something like the following:

```perl
while(1)
{
  ACCEPT_CONNECT:
    {
        ($childsocket = $socket->accept)
            || redo ACCEPT_CONNECT;
    }
    my $pid = fork();
    die "Cannot fork: $!" unless defined($pid);
    if ($pid == 0)
    {
        # Communicate with child socket
    }
}
```

Here I've used fork to create a new process that will be responsible for communicating with the client. After the new process is started, the server will go back to the top of the while loop and wait for new connections.

To communicate with the client you can just use the normal <FILEHANDLE> operator and print function to receive and send data, like so:

```perl
$request = <$childsocket>;
print $childsocket $result;
```

The script on the CD supports a very simple Web server; it only responds to GET requests, but that should be good enough to send simple information back to a browser. By default it works on port 8080, although you can change that easily enough in the script.

If you have problems running the script because it says you are not "root," then you'll need to change the chroot statement at the start of the script. The chroot statement changes the root directory for the script. In this case, you change it to the directory in which the script was run. So if the script is executed in /users/mc, then a request by a Web browser for /index.html will return /users/mc/index.html. The server also won't provide access to /etc/passwd and other sensitive files, because it won't be able to see that directory—as far as the script is concerned, /users/mc *is* the root directory!

Avoiding Deadlock

When communicating between two machines using sockets, potential problems exist concerning the control of the communication between the server and client machines. Provided you are careful, you shouldn't have any difficulties while using the normal print function and <FILEHANDLE> operator. Because Perl treats sockets like filehandles, there is no reason not to use any of the available functions and operators that work with file-handles for transferring information.

That said, it is possible to get into a situation where the client and server both wait for information—a situation otherwise known as deadlock. To avoid deadlock you will need to design a suitable protocol that tells each end of the network link what state it should be in. For basic communication a simple flip-flop scenario should suffice.

That is, the server end waits for data while the client sends information; once transfer is complete, the client end waits for data while the server sends it. Flip-flop is the basic idea behind protocols such as HTTP and SMTP. If you're using one of the standard protocols for client communication, you should probably use the libnet or libwwwperl bundles. See numbers 10, 26, and 27 for some examples.

An alternative solution to deadlock is to open two sockets at each end of the connection. The client opens sockets A and B and then disables sending on A and receiving on B using the shutdown function or method. At the server end, you disable receiving on A and sending on socket B. Now you know which socket to use and check the listening socket's status to determine what to do. Although the alternative improves the situation, you can still enter a deadlocked state if both ends decide to receive data simultaneously.

Many people mistakenly believe that Perl's `select` function eliminates deadlock. It doesn't; all it does is provide a method for a single-threaded process to communicate on more than one socket semi-simultaneously. If both ends of the connection are listening when one of them should be sending, `select` only monitors multiple sockets very efficiently for no data.

30 Accepting Multiple Connections

IO::Select
Built-in
www.perl.com

The socket server in the last number relied on the `fork` function to accept requests from clients. Up until recently, `fork` wouldn't have worked on a Windows machine, because the Windows operating system doesn't support it.

Perl 5.6 fixes the problem; it uses threads to emulate the `fork` mechanism. The approach is less than ideal, and it could present a resource nightmare if the machine suddenly accepts many connections simultaneously.

On either Unix or Windows machines, if 20 people decided to connect within a few seconds, you could have 20 instances of Perl running on your machine, all using memory and CPU resources. You could control the number of connections using a simple counter, but it's still not an ideal solution.

The trick is to accept new connections and then monitor each child socket to see what has been requested. You can use `select` to do so, but it's much easier to use the `IO::Select` module. The `select` module checks for data on each socket, and then, when called, returns an array of filehandles that are either waiting to have data read from them or written to them, or that have an error (such as an end of file).

Setting up IO::Select

Compared to the built-in select function, the IO::Select module is very easy to use. The first stage is to set up the object that will hold the list of file-handles, like so:

```
my $readable = IO::Select->new;
```

Then you just add to the object the filehandles that you want to monitor, using the add method:

```
$readable->add($socket);
```

Note that because you add the filehandle to the IO::Select object, you don't need to keep a separate record of the filehandle elsewhere. The IO::Select module will return a filehandle when it's ready to be used.

Processing the Select Queue

The select method of the IO::Select module, which needs to be called as IO::Select->select() so that it doesn't execute the built-in select function, returns a reference to an array of filehandles that are ready to be processed, either for reading data from or writing data to the sockets. The format of the function is as follows:

```
IO::Select->select(READ, WRITE, ERROR  [, TIMEOUT]);
```

The READ, WRITE, and ERROR arguments should be IO::Select objects that you expect to either be ready for reading, writing, or dealing with an error. The TIMEOUT is the number of seconds to wait for a filehandle to become ready. For example, to process a list of filehandles ready to be read from, you might use something like the following:

```
my ($ready)
    = IO::Select->select($readable, undef, undef, undef);
foreach my $s (@$ready)
{
....
}
```

When dealing with sockets, you add both the server listening socket and the accepted sockets to the object. That way, you can accept new requests and process existing requests without having to separately check the server socket. The script on the CD nicely demonstrates dealing with sockets. Instead of a Web server, the script just returns the status of the server, as determined by the `uptime` command. The connection is not severed once the status has been returned, so you can ask for a status update as many times as you like from as many clients as you like, without having to reconnect.

You can try the server by using `telnet`, like so:

```
$ telnet linux 4000
Trying 198.112.10.135...
Connected to linux.mchome.com.
Escape character is '^]'.
Status server online!
status
Fri Aug 18 17:44:12 2000:   5:44pm  up 23 days,  5:30, 20
  users,  load average: 0.00, 0.00, 0.00
```

Just remember to change the TCP/IP port number, 4000 in this instance, to the port number configured in the server script.

Using IO::Select Instead of fork

One of the problems with `fork` is that it increases resources. With `IO::Select` you needn't spawn new processes to serve new clients, and you're not in any way limited in number of clients you can serve by the server memory resources.

Using `IO::Select` is also in my experience more efficient for servers that return only small amounts of information—just like the server in the script. As the amount of data exchanged increases, however, the efficiency declines because of the "round-robin" approach to servicing the needs of each client. Then `fork` would be more practical.

31 Remote Procedure Calls

RPC::Simple
Dominique Dumont
www.cpan.com

Although the network-communication techniques you've seen in this section are very practical, you will occasionally want a more straightforward way of communicating a simple request and getting a simple response.

Most Unix systems support a system called RPC (Remote Procedure Calls). With RPC you write a set of procedures in a metalanguage, which is then converted into a suite of C routines. Any data is translated into a binary and architecture-neutral format so it can be easily transferred over the network.

When you want to get some information, you only need to call the name of the remote procedure. For example, the rnusers function returns the number of users currently logged into a remote system; to get a simple count you can just use (in C) the following code:

```
count = rnusers('host');
```

Because the RPC system also supports structures, it can be used to transfer quite complex structures. Because the RPC system handles all the communication and translation of information, it takes away all the complication of communicating over a socket and safely transferring data, and leaves you with a very efficient way of getting simple data from a remote machine.

How RPC Works

Remote Procedure Calls work in a very similar way to the object-based interface offered by NET::FTP and other modules. A server waits for a connection from a remote machine. Through the RPC generation service, a suite of RPC functions provides translation to and from the local and remote functions and the necessary communication controls.

When the local machine connects to the remote machine, the following stages take place:

1. The local machine calls the local RPC function.

2. The RPC function translates the arguments supplied into a bytestream, ready for sending over the network.

3. The local machine opens a connection to the remote machine and supplies the function name and the bytestream.

4. The remote machine decodes the bytestream into the arguments that will be supplied to the local version of the function.

5. The remote machine executes the local function.

6. The remote system translates the return values into another bytestream and sends the data back.

7. The local machine decodes the returned bytestring and returns the data to the caller.

Although it's quite a complex process, the only parts of the process you need to worry about are the first and seventh steps—steps 2 through 6 are handled entirely by the RPC libraries.

Under Unix RPC is used for a number of network-level protocols where the need for a full socket-based communication is either impractical or just plain overkill. For example, the rusers service provides information on who is logged into a machine, and rstat gets the information on uptime and current-load levels (just like the uptime command). Even the NIS+ (Network Information Service) uses RPC as a simpler way of authenticating users.

The RPC::Simple Module

Dominique Dumont has produced an RPC system for Perl. Although it doesn't yet provide an interface to the C-based servers already supported under Unix, it does allow you to create a server and client that communicate over a network using a simple object-based interface.

To use the system, you create two object classes, one to handle the remote side and the other to handle the local side. You then pass the object classes off to the RPC system (using the normal inheritance system), which in turn handles all the communication and the transfer of information.

The test script that comes with the RPC::Simple module is probably the best choice to understand how it works. The script uses Tk to provide an interface between the client and server. You can see the output of the script, showing the local and remote query and responses, as follows:

```
$ perl test.pl
1..1
ok 1
spawned server pid 3106
test.pl 3106: server started on port 7810 at Fri Aug 25
11:24:13 2000
Accepting connection
Connection accepted
Comparing 127.0.0.1 with 127.0.0.1
RPC::Simple::Factory object created
creating MyLocal
Creating RPC::Simple::Agent for RealMyLocal.test_pm
test.pl 3106: connection from localhost [ 127.0.0.1 ]  at Fri
Aug 25 11:24:15 2000
creating new RealMyLocal
Remote class RealMyLocal.test_pm created
Remote said 'Hello world'
Local asked me to say hello
implicit answer is Hello local object
...
class MyLocal destroyed
```

By default, the system only supports local connections—i.e., to the 127.0.0.1 localhost address. But you can modify the configuration from your script. Doing so provides a certain level of security, as you can restrict the hosts allowed to execute remote calls. For an even more secure system, consider the Penguin system.

NOTE The RPC::Simple module uses the Tk loop as a way of controlling the asynchronous I/O needed to communicate. You'll need to have installed the Tk module (available from CPAN) in order for the system to work properly.

The Penguin System

Whereas the RPC::Simple module aims to support a set suite of remote procedures that can be executed over a network, Penguin provides a method of executing arbitrary Perl code on a remote machine.

With Penguin any Perl code can be sent and executed on a remote machine running the Penguin daemon. Although you could use it for very simple processing, like the rusers function I discussed earlier, it's actually a much more practical way of running complex processing tasks, such as database queries in a distributed and, more importantly, secure way.

Unlike the RPC system, which really relies only on IP addresses for security, the scripts you send remotely to a Penguin-enabled server are signed and encrypted before transmission. The client and server hold unique signatures, and each end verifies the signature of an incoming transmission to ensure that it's from a trusted source.

Once the source has been verified, the Perl code is decrypted and a new compartment is created (using the Safe module). The new compartment is configured so that it has limited abilities and won't run the risk of executing any code that may upset the remote system. Then the code is executed, and communication between the server and the client continues in this fashion until the whole process is completed and the communication is closed.

Because Penguin relies on the code sent to it for execution, you needn't recreate the server-side procedure calls, as you would have to do with something like RPC::Simple. The security aspect permits you to use Penguin in an environment where you have a secure database server that doesn't allow external communication. Sending and receiving queries could be handled exclusively with Penguin, without exposing the server to the normal barrage of network traffic.

Development Tools

Aside from all the other cool things you can do with Perl, you can also use it to help in the development of your applications. Perl comes with many specific tools that can be cajoled into different roles. Further, certain Perl features you probably didn't realize existed can help to improve your scripts.

32   Profiling Your Perl Scripts

DProf
Built-in
www.perl.com

When you've written the latest solution to a problem, the testing and debugging stages usually follow. The testing phase should be a core part of any program development, as it helps to ensure that the script you have written actually does what you intended. It should also help to highlight anything that the script does that you didn't intend, like overwriting a file.

That's where the debugging comes in; it removes those annoying problems. There's also an additional, sometimes-ignored step, one that I like to include in nearly all my projects. Many would argue that it's not a debugging issue, but I'd disagree.

The final stage of any development should be optimization, the removal of those obstacles and problems that slow your script down but don't actually cause it to fail. The process can take many forms, from simply reducing the number of steps required to achieve a particular goal to changing the way to perform a particular function.

To help the process along, you can use the Perl profiler, actually an extension that replaces the debugger when you start Perl in debugging mode. The profiler monitors the execution of your script, keeping track of the time taken to execute individual function calls. Once the script is complete, it then produces a report that collates all the information and provides a list of the timing for each function.

You can use the information to identify the most processor-intensive functions and attempt to optimize them. It doesn't perform the optimizations for you, but it will help you to identify which functions need attention.

Before you start using the profiler, you may need to make the following adjustments to your script:

◆ When information is retrieved from the user, replace the call with a static piece of data—a wait will skew the results.

◆ If an external application is called, make sure the command is available. Don't substitute the data returned with a static result, because the speed of an external program will affect your script's performance just as much as an internal bug.

◆ If scripts use network sockets, you may want to replace the information sent or received with static data so that you don't introduce network latency into the script's results. Once you are happy that the rest of the script is optimized, go back to using real data and check again.

Profiling a Script

Profiling is a two-stage process:

1. Execute the script using the debugger extensions to call the Dprof module, which in turn produces a file called tmon.out. The file contains all of the timing information in a very raw format.

2. Execute the dprofpp script to parse the tmon.out file and produce the necessary output.

The dprofpp script analyzes the raw data in a number of different ways, so you can run the script once to produce different levels of detail.

To produce the data file, execute a script like so:

```
$ perl -d:DProf test.pl
```

The size of the file produced is directly proportional to the number of function calls made. For the sample script on the CD, you should generate a file about 260K in size.

For a basic profile report, run dprofpp. It will produce a report similar to the following:

```
$ dprofpp
```

```
Total Elapsed Time = -9.21566 Seconds
   User+System Time =         0 Seconds
Exclusive Times
%Time ExclSec CumulS #Calls sec/call Csec/c  Name
 0.00   4.964  2.558 201000   0.0000 0.0000  First::funca
 0.00   4.824  2.418 201000   0.0000 0.0000  First::__ANON__
 0.00   2.847  0.438 201000   0.0000 0.0000  First::funcb
 0.00   1.429  5.104    201   0.0071 0.0254  First::foo
 0.00   0.008  5.103      1   0.0076 5.1034  Second::foo
 0.00   0.000  5.111      1   0.0000 5.1114  main::bar
 0.00   0.000 -0.000      1   0.0000      -  strict::bits
 0.00   0.000 -0.000      1   0.0000      -  strict::import
 0.00   0.000 -0.000      1   0.0000      -  main::BEGIN
```

To get a different report from the dprofpp tool, you need to supply different arguments on the command line. Because the tmon.out file has already been created, you don't need to rerun the script—just have the data reprocessed. You can see a list of the alternative options in the table.

Option	Description
-a	**Sorts the list of subroutines alphabetically.**
-A	**Reports the time for functions loaded via the** AutoLoad **module as** *::AUTOLOAD, **showing the total time for all autoloaded modules. The default is for individual functions (whether autoloaded or not) to have their own time calculated.**
-E	**As the default option, displays all subroutine times exclusive of child subroutine times.**
-F	**Generates fake exit time values. It gets around the problem introduced by subroutines calling** exit or exec, **which causes the normal execution process of the script to end prematurely.**
-g *subroutine*	**Shows only the results for** *subroutine* **and the subroutines it calls.**
-I	**Displays the execution times of child and parent.**
-l	**Sorts the list of subroutines by the number of times each subroutine has been called.**

Option	Description
-O *cnt*	Displays the first *cnt* subroutines; default is 15.
-p *script*	Executes *script* and then outputs report. Still produces the tmon.out **file.**
-Q	Quits after profiling the script with -p, without producing a report.
-q	Displays report without headers.
-R	Individually counts anonymous subroutines within the same package scope. The normal operation is to count each invocation separately.
-r	Displays only the elapsed real times. Individual user and system times are not displayed.
-s	Displays only system times. User times are not displayed.
-S	Displays merged subroutine call tree, with statistical information for each branch, to STDOUT. Making multiple calls to the same function within the same branch creates a new branch at the next level. Repeat counts are displayed for each function within each branch. Sort order is by total time per branch.
-T	Displays subroutine call tree to STDOUT. Statistics are not printed.
-t	Displays subroutine call tree to STDOUT, and subroutines called multiple consecutive times are simply displayed with a repeat count. Statistics are not printed.
-U	Outputs the subroutine list unsorted.
-u	Displays only user times. System times are not displayed.
-V	Prints the version number of the dprofpp **script, and prints the** Devel::Dprof **version number stored in the statistics file if found or specified.**
-v	Sorts by the average time elapsed for child calls within each call.
-z	Sorts the subroutine list by the amount of user and system time used.

Alternatively, if you use the profiler frequently you can populate the DPROFPP_OPTS environment variable to store the default options. The default value used by the profiler is -z -O 15 -E.

For example, you can look at a subroutine tree by using the -S option like so:

```
$ dprofpp -S
main::BEGIN x 1          0.00s = (0.00 + 0.00)s
  strict::import x 1     0.00s = (0.00 + 0.00)s
    strict::bits x 1     0.00s
main::bar x 1    5.11s = (0.00 + 5.11)s
  Second::foo x 1         5.10s = (0.01 + 5.10)s
    First::foo x 200      5.10s = (4.99 + 0.10)s
      First::funca x 1000        0.05s
      First::funcb x 1000        0.04s
      First::__ANON__ x 1000     0.02s
    First::foo x 1        0.01s = (0.00 + 0.03)s
      First::funcb x 1000        0.02s
      First::funca x 1000        0.01s
      First::__ANON__ x 1000     0.00s
```

The subroutine tree shows all the nested calls and how many times they have been executed. Note that the strict module import incurs no overhead (it's got no significant Perl code to be executed), and that anonymous functions are lumped together into a single __ANON__ entity. You can instead use the –R function to count the anonymous functions individually.

33 Using the Compiler for More Than Compiling

B and 0 modules
Built-in
www.perl.com

Did you know that you could compile your Perl scripts into stand-alone applications, just like a normal C/C++-based stand-alone application?

The Perl compiler is one of the more unusual parts of the Perl system that has recently started to have an effect on the Perl community. Its primary purpose is to enable you to convert a Perl script into stand-alone C source and then compile that file into a final executable. (You can use the compiler for some other, less obvious purposes.)

In fact, it doesn't actually do exactly what it sounds like it would. The system doesn't convert the Perl source into C source; instead, it embeds a compiled version of the Perl source code into a C source file. Once compiled, the C application calls the Perl interpreter and gets it to execute the compiled Perl script directly, thereby ignoring the compilation stage altogether.

In order to understand how the system works, you have to understand how Perl scripts are executed. Without going into too much detail here, Perl scripts are optimized and compiled into a series of opcodes—much like assembler code. It's these opcodes and the corresponding tree that are executed by the Perl "virtual machine," the actual execution element of the interpreter. The same virtual-machine concept is used by other languages like Python and Java.

This compilation/execution stage provides all the benefits of a scripted language; it allows for source files to be executed directly, but with the optimization effects of a compiled language. The optimization and compilation process does much work to remove duplications and produce a reasonable level of optimization without costing too much initialization time during program execution.

Because the opcodes are very simple, they can be described by a series of bytecodes, essentially similar to the machine codes used by a physical CPU for execution, except in this case they're bytecodes for the virtual machine instead. Bytecode has some advantages over the raw-text script. Beyond the size and optimization implications, it's difficult but not impossible to resolve the bytecode into its original text, although certain aspects, such as variable names, are lost.

You can save the optimized bytecode into a file that can be executed directly. This can be useful in some situations where you are trying to protect the source code from being copied by its end users.

The most useful feature of opcodes is that because the tree can be executed directly, you could remove the compilation stage when executing the script. In time-critical applications such as Web sites, skipping the stage can save minutes, even hours, of the cumulative compilation time involved in executing the same script a number of times. Skipping the stage can also improve the overall Web response times.

The time taken to load, optimize, and compile a script is milliseconds, but on a Web site that executes the same script thousands of times in a day, you can see the savings. PerlEx (available for ActivePerl) and the `mod_perl` extension for Apache skip the compilation stage (they store the precompiled bytecode) and therefore do all the optimization work for you.

How the Compiler Works

The compiler, in a sense, does less work than the normally used interpreter does. Whereas both programs resolve the source code to a series of bytecodes, the compiler doesn't take the next step of execution. Instead, using a series of "backends," it can write them in a variety of formats, for example as C source code, parsing trees, a regurgitated script (i.e., a text version of the script as it was interpreted, rather than as you wrote it), and even the raw bytecode itself. The C source code can subsequently be compiled using `gcc` or a similar C compiler.

The Perl interpreter (rather than the compiler) follows the basic sequence as shown:

1. Read the source code.

2. Resolve the source code into a series of opcodes (the smallest executable element of a Perl script) and a corresponding opcode tree that describes the execution path.

3. Optimize the opcode tree. The interpreter may remove or combine opcodes into single statements (e.g., changing the static calculation 4+4, which uses three opcodes, into the constant value 8, which uses only one) to produce the final optimized tree.

4. Execute the opcode tree.

The Perl compiler takes the interpreted code either at the end of stage 2 or 3, depending on whether you want to use optimized code or not.

The information about a script is determined by the B module, which in turn uses a number of additional modules to turn that information into the C source code, raw bytecode, or other forms. The backends generally take the opcode tree at either stage 2 or 3. You can see a list of the backends available with Perl 5.6 in the table.

Backend	Description
C	Creates C source with the embedded Perl bytecode and the necessary code to import and execute the code using the Perl interpreter.
CC	Creates C source based on an optimized version of the Perl source file. The source is essentially identical to the format in which a script would be executed by the interpreter, but it still employs the bytecode principle. The code is based on a complex switch statement sequence written in C, which in turn calls the necessary bytecode instructions to manipulate Perl data types. Thus the resulting code is a C/Perl hybrid. You are not modifying C variables or using raw C interpretations of the Perl code.
Bytecode	Produces raw bytecode using the optimized version of the script. The bytecode is architecture neutral and can be executed directly by the ByteLoader module.
Debug	Outputs a complete and verbose opcode tree to STDOUT. Debug is usually only of any use to opcode junkies and backend developers.
Terse	A reduced version of Debug, outputting a less verbose opcode tree.
Xref	Reports the declaration and use of the subroutines and variables within your script. It is useful for tracking the execution of certain elements in your scripts.
Lint	On certain elements performs tests more stringent than either switching on warnings or using the strict pragma.
Deparse	Regurgitates the Perl script in the format in which Perl interpreted it. It has the effect of producing a slightly optimized and reformatted version of the script, taking into account operator precedence. Aside from some formatting and optimization, the script should look identical to your original— provided your script passes through the interpreter OK.
ShowLex	Generates a list of variables declared using the my keyword from your script.

I'll ignore the C, CC, and Bytecode backends and instead look at how some of the other backends can be used to investigate your script more fully.

Terse Backend

The Terse backend is useful when you want to examine the compiled opcode tree of a script. Although it only provides very basic information, it should be enough for you to follow what is happening in your scripts. Consider the following great example of what Terse shows—the output of the statement $a = $b + 2;:

```
$ perl -MO=Terse -e '$a = $b + 2;'
LISTOP (0x81b2dc0) leave
    OP (0x81b2de8) enter
    COP (0x81b2d88) nextstate
    BINOP (0x81b2d60) sassign
        BINOP (0x81b2d38) add [1]
            UNOP (0x81b2cf8) null [15]
                SVOP (0x8141930) gvsv  GV (0x81414d8) *b
            SVOP (0x81b2d18) const  IV (0x8136c38) 2
        UNOP (0x81b1c88) null [15]
            SVOP (0x81b4488) gvsv  GV (0x814146c) *a
-e syntax OK
```

You can see here three scalar variables (SVOPs), one for each of the components in the calculation. They are nested within a simple binary operation, add; the rest of the code is simply preamble before you reach that execution stage.

You can use Terse to examine the optimizations made by Perl during the compilation stage. To demonstrate the reduction optimization, consider the calculation $a = 2 + 2;:

```
$ perl -MO=Terse -e '$a = 2 + 2;'
LISTOP (0x81b2cc8) leave
    OP (0x81b2cf0) enter
    COP (0x81b2c90) nextstate
    BINOP (0x81b2c68) sassign
        SVOP (0x8141930) const  IV (0x8141520) 4
        UNOP (0x81b1c88) null [15]
            SVOP (0x81b4488) gvsv  GV (0x814146c) *a
-e syntax OK
```

You can see how silly a simple calculation like that is when included in a script. It's actually resolved to a single scalar value of four before the script is executed, helping to improve performance. Although it's unlikely you'll perform such simple calculations internally, it's a useful way of examining exactly what optimizations do take place and where you can improve your script.

Similar optimizations take place on strings:

```
perl -MO=Terse -e '$a = "hello " . "world";'
LISTOP (0x81b2cd0) leave
    OP (0x81b2cf8) enter
    COP (0x81b2c98) nextstate
    BINOP (0x81b2c70) sassign
        SVOP (0x8141938) const  PV (0x8136c38) "hello world"
        UNOP (0x81b1c90) null [15]
            SVOP (0x81b4490) gvsv  GV (0x8141474) *a
-e syntax OK
```

The problem with the foregoing format is that it's shown in opcode-tree order, which is not necessarily execution order. To get around the problem you can supply the exec option to the Terse backend:

```
$ perl -MO=Terse,exec -e '$a = $b + 2;'
OP (0x40013c10) enter
COP (0x400956c0) nextstate
SVOP (0x4008a9e0) gvsv  GV (0x4001a0ac) *b
SVOP (0x400a86a0) const  IV (0x4000c1f0) 2
BINOP (0x400a8680) add [1]
SVOP (0x4000e220) gvsv  GV (0x4001a040) *a
BINOP (0x400a8660) sassign
LISTOP (0x400a48e0) leave
-e syntax OK
```

You lose much of the information structure, but the sequence of execution is much clearer. You can use the output to check the precedence order of a statement. Alternatively, you can use the Deparse backend.

Deparse Backend

The Deparse backend is probably my favorite; just before a script is to be executed, it regurgitates the version of it as it was interpreted. Unlike the

Terse and other backends, the information is produced in the form of a script that you could supply to Perl directly. In effect, it produces a "perfect" version of the script in its optimized and understood state.

For example, look at the output of a one-line foreach statement:

```
$perl -MO=Deparse -e 'foreach (reverse sort keys %main::) {
print }'
foreach $_ (reverse sort(keys %main::)) {
    print $_;
}
```

You can see here that it regurgitates the loop separating the lines, including the implied $_ calls, and places parentheses around the sort function to make the precedence clearer.

Xref Backend

The Xref backend provides the same basic functionality as the xref tool available for C. It produces a report that lists functions and variables and where they are defined and used within the script. You can use this information either as a simple development aid or as a way of debugging your code by examining which functions are modifying a particular variable.

Line numbers may be prefixed with a letter to indicate the reference type. You can see the list of valid letters in the table.

Prefix	Description
i	Indicates a lexical variable has been introduced.
&	Function or method call.
s	Function definition.
r	Format definition.

With Xref you can, for example, get a better overview of the test script used in the last chapter and get much more detail about functions and variables than even the profiler produces, as shown:

```
$ perl -MO=Xref test.pl
File test.pl
```

```
Subroutine (definitions)
  Package First
    &foo              s19
    &funca            s7
    &funcb            s8
  Package Second
    &foo              s31
  Package UNIVERSAL
    &VERSION          s0
    &can              s0
    &isa              s0
  Package attributes
    &bootstrap        s0
  Package main
    &bar              s39
Subroutine (main)
  Package (lexical)
    $funcc            i10
  Package main
    &bar              &41
Subroutine First::foo
  Package (lexical)
    $funcc            &15, 15
    $i                i14, 15, 15, 15, 15, 15
  Package First
    &funca            &15
    &funcb            &15
Subroutine Second::foo
  Package (lexical)
    $i                i25, 26, 28, 29, 26
    $j                i25
  Package First
    &foo              &29
Subroutine bar
  Package First
    &foo              &38
  Package Second
    &foo              &37
test.pl syntax OK
```

You can tell from the listing that the $i variable is created on line 14 and then used in line 15 within the First::foo function. Within the Second::foo function it's created on line 25 and then used in lines 26, 28, and 29. Also note that it gives a breakdown according to packages as well as functions, so you can see that a foo function is created and used from both the First and Second packages.

34 Writing Perl XtenSions

h2xs
Built-in
www.perl.com

Many of the modules that I've discussed make use of Perl extensions—pieces of C source code used to augment the abilities of Perl. Although Perl is a very practical and capable language, it doesn't contain the inherent ability to talk directly to an external C library. Instead, you need to write an extension module that provides the glue code to sit between Perl and the C function or library. The glue code provides the necessary conversion routines to translate C data types into their internal Perl equivalent.

You may think such a task is quite difficult. But it's actually easier than it appears, especially if you use the h2xs utility provided with Perl to build many of the files you need. The glue code is written in a metalanguage (commonly known as XS) that defines a number of XSUBs—that is, eXtension SUBroutines.

The h2xs utility is the easiest way to start. It's primarily designed to convert a C header file into suitable XS stub that can then be used to interface between Perl and your C code. However, in addition to the XS definition file, it also produces a number of basic items that you should include with all modules.

Among the items is a Perl Makefile that will produce a traditional Makefile that in turn can compile and install your module into your Perl installation directory. The h2xs utility also creates a Perl script that you can use for testing, and the template module file, which even includes template POD documentation.

Using the h2xs Tool

In its base format, the h2xs tool will only convert the constant definitions in the header file into Perl constants. You still have to manually update the XS file to provide the functional interface between the C library and the Perl module you are creating. The basic format for the command is as follows:

```
h2xs [-AOPXcdfh] [-v version] [-n module_name] [-p prefix] [-s
subs] [headerfile [extra_libraries]]
```

The command-line options are described in the table.

Option	Description
-A	**Omit the autoloading definitions (implies the** -c **option)**
-F	**Additional flags for C preprocessor (used with** -x**)**
-O	**Allow overwriting of a preexisting extension directory**
-P	**Omit the stub POD section**
-X	**Omit the XS portion**
-c	**Omit the** constant() **function and specialized AUTOLOAD from the XS file**
-d	**Turn on debugging messages**
-f	**Force creation of the extension**
-n	**Specify a name to use for the extension—defaults to a title-case version of the header file's basename**
-p	**Specify a string that will be removed from the start of the C functions when they are reproduced as Perl functions**
-s	**Create subroutines for specified macros**
-v	**Specify a version number for this extension**
-x	**Autogenerate XSUBs using** C::Scan

To convert the math library installed under Unix, you might use the following:

```
$ h2xs -n MyMath /usr/include/math.h -lm
Writing MyMath/MyMath.pm
Writing MyMath/MyMath.xs
Writing MyMath/Makefile.PL
Writing MyMath/test.pl
Writing MyMath/Changes
Writing MyMath/MANIFEST
```

The easiest way to use the h2xs tool is to install the C::Scan module (available from CPAN), which will do its best to produce the necessary XS definitions based on the function definitions in the header file, as shown:

```
$ h2xs -x -n MyMath /usr/include/math.h -lm
Scanning typemaps...
  Scanning /usr/local/lib/perl5/5.6.0/ExtUtils/typemap
Scanning /usr/include/math.h for functions...
Writing MyMath/MyMath.pm
Writing MyMath/MyMath.xs
Writing MyMath/typemap
Writing MyMath/Makefile.PL
Writing MyMath/test.pl
Writing MyMath/Changes
Writing MyMath/MANIFEST
```

Once it's completed writing out the files to your new module directory, all you need to do is follow the same basic procedure as for installing any other Perl module. That is:

```
$ perl Makefile.PL
$ make
$ make test
$ make install
```

Then, at least in theory, everything should work!

Writing your own XS stubs

Although the h2xs and C::Scan tools will do their best, they are only designed to handle the standard data types, such as int and float. When it comes to more complex structures, such as arrays and struct or union structures, the tools start to fall down. They can't automatically determine how to translate between the complex formats and the simple stack system employed by Perl for exchanging information.

In these situations you'll have to write your own XS stubs. I don't have the space to delve into too much detail here, but I will look at the basic layout. For more information, check the perlxs manual page.

To create an "empty" module—that is, one that doesn't have any pre-defined functions—and just a blank XS file stub, use the -c option to the h2xs utility, as shown:

```
$ h2xs -c -n MyModule
```

Here's a very simple XS definition that includes the function within the code:

```
int
add(a,b)
        int a
        int b
        CODE:
                RETVAL = a+b;
        OUTPUT:
                RETVAL
```

The first line is the return type—Perl will automatically convert it to a scalar. The next line defines the function name and the argument it accepts. The next two lines define the data types for the arguments. Again, Perl (through the XS system) will translate a Perl scalar into C integers. The CODE block contains the code that will make up the function Perl will call when you use the add function in your script. The special RETVAL is the name given to the return value that will be returned by the Perl function. Add it to the end of a blank XS file and then compile the module.

You can then start using the new C function from within Perl. It's easy, as shown:

```
$ perl -MSmath -e 'print add(1,2)'
```

Here's another XS definition, this time for a function that returns the number of bytes available on a file system. It uses the statvfs function to obtain the data and then computes a result, returning it as a long, which the XS system will convert to a Perl scalar for you. Consider the following:

```
long
fsavail (path)
```

```
            char *  path
            CODE:
                    struct statvfs vfsrec;
                    int statreturn;
                    statreturn = statvfs(path,&vfsrec);
                    if (statreturn == 0)
                    {
                        RETVAL = (vfsrec.f_frsize * \
                                vfsrec.f_bavail);
                    }
                    else
                    {
                        RETVAL = -1;
                    }
            OUTPUT:
            RETVAL
```

For more complicated interfaces, you need to communicate with the Perl interpreter by placing, or indeed obtaining, information from the Perl argument stack, which is used to communicate information between function calls. See the documentation for more information.

35 Installing Modules from CPAN

CPAN
Built-in
www.perl.com

Throughout this book I've looked at a combination of Perl tricks using built-in functions, supplied libraries, and a selection of the extensions and libraries available from CPAN. CPAN stands for the Comprehensive Perl Archive Network and is a central repository for the modules that make up the Perl library. The archive includes not only extension modules, but also the core library modules supplied with Perl, and the latest versions of Perl.

CPAN provides a comprehensive reference point for keeping your Perl installation up-to-date. As bugs are fixed and new features are added to the different modules, they are uploaded to CPAN and available for installation. Keeping up with such information by hand is difficult, if not impossible, when you use anything beyond the standard Perl distribution.

The solution is to use the CPAN module included with Perl. It provides a command-line interface for interactively downloading and installing modules. Within the shell you can search for modules matching a particular expression, install modules, and even determine the list of modules that need to be updated. The programmable interface provides the same functionality but enables you to automate the process you would follow within the shell.

Irrespective of the interface you use, the CPAN module will take into account any modules required by the one you are trying to install. So you can leave it up to CPAN to install everything you need to start working with a particular module.

The CPAN module even downloads modules from your local repository for you. It makes use of the Net::FTP or LWP modules if they are available, or it uses the lynx Web browser and even an external ftp client to download the information and modules it needs.

The CPAN module therefore takes out much of the manual work otherwise required when downloading and installing a module from the CPAN library. It is probably the best way to download modules from CPAN, as it guarantees that you will get the latest version and ensures that any required modules will also be downloaded and installed.

To get the best out of CPAN, you should do at least the following:

◆ Run through the interactive shell and configure the CPAN module first. You can force it by running:

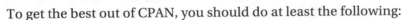

```
$ perl -MCPAN::FirstTime -e CPAN::FirstTime::init
```

◆ Choose the CPAN site closest to you; most ISPs provide a hosting service for CPAN modules.

◆ Install the libnet bundle as soon as possible, because it will improve the chances of you successfully downloading the files CPAN needs.

Interactive Shell Interface

The shell interface, also known as interactive mode, puts Perl into a simple shell-style interface. The first time the shell interface runs, you will go through a configuration process that sets up your environment for using the CPAN module. The process includes configuration of the internal system used to access raw data from the Internet, your preferred download location, and proxy information.

The shell interface supports the commands listed in the table. You can use the shell to query the CPAN archives and also to download and install modules.

Command	Arguments	Description
a	*EXPR*	**Searches the list of authors.** *EXPR* **should be a simple string, in which case a search will be made for an exact match with the author's ID. Alternatively, you can supply a regular expression that will search for matching author IDs and name details.**
b		**Displays a list of the bundles of modules—for example, the** LWP **and** libnet **extensions are available as a bundle, as are some collections of the** DBI **and** DBD **interfaces.**
d	*EXPR*	**Performs a regular-expression search for a package/module.**
m	*EXPR*	**Displays information about the expression matching** *EXPR*.
i	*EXPR*	**Displays information about a module, bundle, or user specified in** *EXPR*.
r	*EXPR*	**Displays a list of reinstallation recommendations, comparing the existing module list against installed modules and versions. If** *EXPR* **is not specified, it lists all recommendations.**
u	*EXPR*	**Lists all modules not currently installed but available on CPAN.**

Command	Arguments	Description
make	*EXPR*	**Downloads the module specified in** *EXPR*, **builds it, and installs it. No check is performed to ensure that you need to install the module—it just does it. Use** install **if you want to update a module based on its version number.**
test	*EXPR*	**Runs** make test **on the module specified in** *EXPR*.
install	*EXPR*	**Downloads and installs the module specified in** *EXPR*. **Runs** make install. **If** *EXPR* **is a module, then it checks to see if the currently installed version of the module specified in** *EXPR* **is lower than that available on CPAN. If it is, it downloads, builds, and installs it. If** *EXPR* **is a distribution file, then the file is processed without any version checking.**
clean	*EXPR*	**Runs a** make clean **on the specified module.**
force	make|test| install *EXPR*	**Forces a** make, test, **or** install **on a command within the current session. Normally, modules are not rebuilt or installed within the current session.**
readme		**Displays the README file.**
reload	index|cpan	**Loads the most recent CPAN index files, or the latest version of the** CPAN **module.**
h|?		**Displays the help menu.**
o		**Gets and sets the various configuration options for the** CPAN **module.**
!	*EXPR*	**Evaluates the Perl expression** *EXPR*.
q		**Quits the interactive shell.**

To install a module with the interactive shell, the easiest method is to use the install command, as shown:

```
$ perl -MCPAN -e shell
cpan> install Nice
```

To install a CPAN bundle:

```
cpan> install Bundle::LWP
Fetching with Net::FTP:

  ftp://ftp.demon.co.uk/pub/mirrors/perl/CPAN/authors/id/GAAS/
libwww-perl-5.42.tar.gz

  CPAN: MD5 security checks disabled because MD5 not installed.
  Please consider installing the MD5 module.

x libwww-perl-5.42/, 0 bytes, 0 tape blocks
x libwww-perl-5.42/t/, 0 bytes, 0 tape blocks
x libwww-perl-5.42/t/net/, 0 bytes, 0 tape blocks
x libwww-perl-5.42/t/net/cgi-bin/, 0 bytes, 0 tape blocks
x libwww-perl-5.42/t/net/cgi-bin/test, 526 bytes, 2 tape blocks
...
```

Programmable Interface

Depending on what you are trying to achieve, you might find the programmable interface to be more useful. All of the commands available in the interactive shell are also available as CPAN::Shell methods within any Perl script. The methods take the same arguments as their shell-interface equivalents.

Individual methods are identical to their command equivalents, but instead of outputting a list to STDOUT, the methods return a list of suitable IDs for the corresponding entity type. You can thus combine individual methods into entire statements, which is not available in the shell. For example, the following will reinstall all the outdated modules currently installed:

```
$ perl -MCPAN -e 'CPAN::Shell->install(CPAN::Shell->r)'
```

The CPAN::Shell module also supports a further function, called expand. The following code returns an array of CPAN::Module objects expanded according to their correct type:

```
expand(TYPE, LIST)
```

The TYPE is the type of object to expand; for example, "Module" or "Author." The LIST is the list of entries to expand. For example, you can expand and install a number of modules at once, using the code shown here:

```
for $module (qw/Bundle::libnet Bundle::LWP/)
{
    my $object = CPAN::Shell->expand('Module',$module);
    $object->install;
}
```

The script on the CD uses the programmable interface to build up a list of extensions installed on a platform and then uses the file and the script to install those modules onto a platform. I've used this script on a site that needed a specific set of modules to support a Web site. By setting up one machine with all the modules I needed, I just used the script to install the same set onto each machine in the network.

To use the script, extract the list of installed modules. Perl stores the information about installed modules in the perllocal.pod file stored in the architecture-specific directory within the Perl library directory. The script gets the information from that file and builds a list of modules. You can extract the list like so:

```
$ cpaninst.pl -c
Created local.mod with a list of machine specific modules
```

Now copy the local.mod file and the script to a new machine and code the following:

```
$ cpaninst.pl -i
```

That code will install all the modules installed on the previous platform. Keep the files hanging around, and you can update them with the -u option. The cpanist.pl script only updates the additional modules installed, not all of the modules installed on the system.

The last option does not specify anything. The script will list all of the additional modules installed and compare the installed version numbers with the numbers registered on CPAN. The following listing is an example:

```
$ cpaninst.pl
Module DBI::FAQ could do with updating, currently 0.37, should
be 0.38
```

```
Module GD::Graph could do with updating, currently 1.24, should
be 1.32
Module Heap could do with updating, currently 0.01, should be
0.50
Module Math::Currency could do with updating, currently 0.03,
should be 0.06
Module Test could do with updating, currently 1.13, should be
1.14
Module Tie::Handle could do with updating, currently 1.0,
should be 3.0
Module URI could do with updating, currently 1.05, should be
1.06
```

36 Writing POD Documentation

Larry Wall
`www.perl.com`

There is a huge variety of documentation formats out there, from those supported directly under Unix, such as `nroff` and TEX, to Windows help files, and to the older MacOS help system, which used a proprietary format. In addition, other more architecture-neutral formats are available, such as HTML, PostScript, and Acrobat PDFs.

Perl is a cross-platform language, so using an architecture-specific format is not an option. A more neutral format such as HTML causes its own problems on machines where it may be possible, but not necessarily practical, to have an HTML browser around all the time. Instead, Perl documentation is written in Plain Old Documentation (POD) format. It's a text-based format that uses a similar tag-based system as HTML, but the overall format is much simpler. It can be viewed directly by a number of Perl tools and by the Shuck application on the Mac.

Because POD is very simple, it can also be easily translated into other formats. POD is automatically translated into `nroff` under Unix and HTML under Windows. Perl even comes with the tools to allow you to convert the documentation yourself.

POD Components

The POD format works somewhat differently than HTML, even though it uses the same basic premise of simple text tabs. A POD document consists of different paragraph types: verbatim, command, and ordinary text. The purpose of each paragraph type is fixed in terms of the POD documentation but unique when translated.

The translation of the paragraph information is up to the translation script that turns the original POD documentation into its final state. For example, ordinary paragraphs are turned into justified-text paragraphs when converted to text but embedded into paragraph tags when converted to HTML.

Each element can also have embedded escape sequences that allow you to specify an alternative printed format for a word or sentence, such as boldface and underline. You can also introduce references and links to other documents or other parts of the same document, just like HTML. Again, it's up to the translation scripts to convert the embedded tags into the corresponding format. For HTML the embedded tags become a clickable link, and for Unix manual pages (as available through the man command), they become underlined references.

No standard format or layout for a POD document exists, but different translators place certain levels of significance on different elements within the source POD file. For example, the text translator ignores links. You'll have a look at a sample document shortly, but remember that all the different encoding samples can be used to create some very simple documentation with little effort.

Command Paragraph

Command paragraphs specify that some special element or formatting should be applied to the supplied word, sentence, paragraph, or section. It allows you to insert headings, subheadings, and lists into the document. All command paragraphs start with an equal sign and a keyword that specifies the formatting to be applied. The paragraph may include an additional keyword or reference. For example, the following paragraph creates a level-one heading, the text of which is "This is a main heading." Other command paragraphs are shown in the table.

```
=head1 This is a main heading
```

Command	Result
=head1 *text*	Applies first-level heading, using "text" as the description.
=head2 *text*	Applies second-level heading, using "text" as the description.
=over *n*	Starts indentation of paragraphs with n specifying the number of characters to use for indentation. End the indentation with =back.
=item *text*	Specifies the title for an item in a list. The value of text will be interpreted differently, according to the translator.
=back	Ends a list/indentation.
=for *format*	Allows you to specify that the following paragraph should be inserted exactly as supplied, according to the specified format. For example, the code here would be inserted into the translated file only by an HTML translator: =for html <font size=+1>Heading</font>
=begin *format* =end *format*	Acts similarly to =for, except that all the paragraphs between =begin and =end are included by the specified format translator as preformatted text.
=pod	Specifies the start of a POD document. It is best used when the documentation is included as part of a script. The =pod command paragraph tells the compiler to ignore the following text.
=cut	Specifies the end of a =pod section.

Of all the command paragraphs, the head paragraphs are the most important, as they help to define the major and minor headings within the document.

Some accepted standards govern the layout of the individual components of your document. At the top level (indicated by =head1) are the major sections of the document, such as the title or synopsis of the POD document. The second level consists of the subheadings, perhaps major components or functions. If you need an additional level beyond the first two, you can use =item entries to add new levels. Just use it in combination with the =over command paragraph to indent each additional heading.

The following table lists, in the rough order in which they should appear, the major headings you should include for all POD documentation. You don't have to include all of the elements—don't include a bugs heading if there aren't any, for example—but you should include the NAME, SYNOPSIS, DESCRIPTION, and AUTHOR sections, especially if you are aiming to release the code and its document to the public.

Element	Description
NAME	Mandatory, comma-separated list of the functions or programs documented by the man page
SYNOPSIS	Outline of the function's or program's purpose
DESCRIPTION	Longer description/discussion of the program's purpose
OPTIONS	The command-line options or function arguments
RETURN VALUE	What the program returns if successful
ERRORS	Any return codes, errors, or exceptions that may be produced
EXAMPLES	Examples of the program's or function's use
ENVIRONMENT	The environment or variables used by and modified by the program
FILES	The files used
SEE ALSO	Other entries to refer to
NOTES	Any additional commentary
CAVEATS/WARNINGS	Anything to be aware of during the program's use
DIAGNOSTICS	Errors or messages produced by the program and what they mean
BUGS	Things that do not work as expected
RESTRICTIONS	Items that are built-in design features and limitations
AUTHOR	Who wrote the function or program
HISTORY	The source or origin of the program or function

Ordinary Text Paragraph

Ordinary paragraphs of text are justified and filled during the translation process according to the destination format. How the justification takes place is entirely dependent on the translator and the reader of the file it creates.

Verbatim Paragraph

A verbatim paragraph will be reproduced within the final document exactly; you cannot use formatting escapes, and the translator won't make any assumptions about the contents of the paragraph. A verbatim paragraph is identified by indentation in the source text, either with spaces or tabs. The best use for a verbatim paragraph is to reproduce code within the document to ensure that it appears as working code within the final document. Without this facility the code would be justified and filled just like any other paragraph.

Escape Sequences

Escape sequences are recognized within both ordinary text and command paragraphs, and they allow you to specify that a block of text is to be displayed as italicized, boldfaced, underlined, and so on. An escape sequence consists of a single letter and a pair of angle brackets that contain the text to be modified. For example, the following POD fragment specifies that the string should be boldfaced:

```
B<Hello World!>
```

It produces:

```
Hello World!
```

Other escape sequences include links to other types of documents and insertion of literal (nontranslated) text elements. How the escape sequences are interpreted is again up to the translation and destination format—some will be ignored, and others will imply that additional information will be added to the embedded sequence.

The first table provides a list of the escape sequences supported by the POD format.

Sequence	Description
I<*text*>	Italic text.
B<*text*>	Boldfaced text.
S<*text*>	Text with nonbreaking spaces (spaces within text that will not be used to wrap or split lines).
C<*code*>	Literal code fragment (for example, the C <printf()> function).
L<*name*>	A link or cross-reference to another section, identified by name. See the next table.
F<*file*>	Used for file names.
X<*index*>	An index entry.
Z<>	A zero-width character.
E<*escape*>	A named character (similar to HTML escapes).
E<lt>	A literal <.
E<gt>	A literal >.
E<*n*>	Character number (in ASCII).

The second table lists the link-specific interpretations.

Sequence	Description
L<*name*>	Manual page
L<*name*/*ident*>	Item or section within a manual page
L<*name*/"*sec*">	Section in another manual page
L<"*sec*">	Section within the current manual page (quotes are optional, as in L<*name*>)

Sequence	Description
L</"sec">	Same as above
L<text|name> L<text|name/ident> L<text|name/"sec"> L<text|"sec"> L<text|/"sec">	Same as above, but destination is identified by name but displayed as text; the text element cannot contain | or >

Embedding Documentation

Unlike most other forms of documentation, Perl allows you to embed POD-formatted sequences directly into your Perl source code. It is not really new; other systems have allowed it, but generally only as part of the header or footer to the script or module. Perl allows you to embed sequences at will anywhere within your code, so you can document a function where the function is defined within the code, which is useful as a cross-reference.

The embedding process keys on a command paragraph, and all text after that is taken as POD documentation until the interpreter sees the =cut command paragraph. The opposite is used by the POD translators: they ignore the Perl script and only work on the POD documentation sequences.

For example, when documenting two functions you might use the following:

```
=item * add function

Adds two numbers together.

=cut

sub add
{
    $_[0]+$_[1];
}

=item * subtract function
```

```
Subtracts the second number from the first.

=cut

sub subtract
{
    $_[0] -$_[1];
}
```

The code does nothing when executed as a Perl script (except for defining two functions that you never use!). But if you convert it to another format and view the document, you see a nicely formatted document. The following graphic shows a sample of the previous code formatted and displayed within Shuck, the Mac POD file viewer.

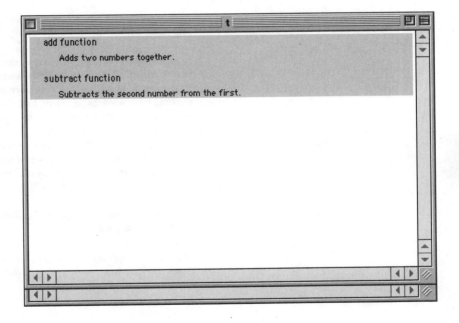

Conversion to Other Formats

It should be obvious by now that POD documentation by itself is fairly useless. It can't be viewed and easily understood without a great deal of effort, and no POD reader exists (unless you have a Mac that can use the Shuck application).

Before POD documents can be useful, you therefore need to use a translator to convert them into something you can read. The base Perl distribution comes with stand-alone tools for converting POD documentation into text, HTML, and Unix man pages (`nroff`), all of which are supported by a series of modules.

You can also download a number of additional modules from CPAN that help convert to other formats or provide POD-related utilities. You can see a sampling in the table.

Module	Description
Pod::DocBook	**Translates to the SGML-based DocBook format.**
Pod::Html	**Translates for HTML documents, supplied as part of the standard library.**
Pod::Man	**Converts to the man-based** `nroff` **format. It is a supplied module.**
Pod::PlainText	**Translates to raw, plain text, essentially stripping all the formatting from the POD document. Paragraphs are justified and attempts are made to make the conversion clear, but it doesn't attempt the same sort of formatting as** `Pod::Text`.
Pod::RTF	**Converts to RTF (Rich Text Format) files. RTF files can be imported and formatted in most word processors, including Microsoft Word, Sun's StarOffice, and Lotus WordPro.**
Pod::SimpleText	**Converts to the SimpleText format used on the Mac for README files.**
Pod::Text	**Supports terminal formatting on suitable devices. It is a supplied text-conversion module.**
Pod::Text::Color	**As an extension, allows POD documents to be formatted and viewed using color-based formatting.**
Pod::Text::Termcap	**As an extension, makes use of the terminal abilities for bold and underlining on terminals that support it.**

Text

If you do not want to view formatted output from a POD document, you can convert it into text format. The resulting output is not completely without format, and the capabilities of your display are taken into account during the translation process. The Pod::Text module provides the capabilities you need, and the base distribution includes a command-line interface to the module in the form of the pod2text script. Consider the following:

```
$ pod2text [-a] [-width] script.pl
```

The script takes only one argument—the name of the file to translate. The resulting text will be sent to STDOUT after it has been converted. There are two additional, optional arguments. The -a argument assumes an alternative, and in fact less capable, terminal. It removes more of the POD formatting but is useful on terminals that don't support the formatting. (See also the Pod::PlainText module.) The *width* argument specifies the width of the output device, where *width* is the width in characters.

HTML

The most compatible destination format (especially across platforms) is HTML. The pod2html script works in the same way as the pod2text script, as shown:

```
$ pod2html script.pl
```

Output is also sent to STDOUT, so you will need to redirect the generated HTML to a file if you want to install it on a Web server or view it with a browser.

You can also write scripts that programmatically use the Pod::Html module, which exports a single function, pod2html. The pod2html function accepts the same arguments as the stand-alone script; you just supply them as you would on the command line, as follows:

```
pod2html("--infile=Module.pm","--netscape");
```

You can see a list of the supported arguments in the table. I'll look at an example of converting POD files in number 37.

Option	Description
--flush	Flushes the contents of the item and directory caches created during the parsing of a POD document.
--help	Prints out a help message.
--htmlroot	Specifies the base directory from which you reference documents relatively. The argument is required if you expect to install the generated HTML files on a Web server. The default is "/."
--index	Inserts an index of =head1 elements at the top of the HTML file generated (default).
--infile	Specifies the file name to convert. You don't have to use this element; the first unhyphenated argument is taken as a filename. If you don't specify a file by either method, then input will be taken from standard input.
--libpods	Holds a colon-separated list of pages searched when referencing =item entries. The list doesn't consist of the file names—just the page names, as they would appear in L<> link elements.
--netscape	Specifies the use of Netscape-specific browser directives when necessary.
--nonetscape	Prevents the use of Netscape-specific browser directives (default).
--outfile	Specifies the destination file name for the generated HTML. Uses standard output if none is specified.
--podpath	Holds a colon-separated list of directories containing POD files and libraries.
--podroot	Specifies the base directory attached to the beginning of each entry in the podpath command-line argument. The default is "." (dot)—the current directory.
--noindex	Stipulates not to generate an index at the top of the HTML file created.
--norecurse	Stipulates no recursion into the subdirectories specified in the podpath option.

Option	Description
`--recurse`	**Stipulates recursion into the subdirectories specified in the** `podpath` **option (default).**
`--title`	**Holds the contents of the** `<TITLE>` **tag in the created HTML document.**
`--verbose`	**Produces status and progress messages during production.**

Unix "man" Pages

The online documentation on Unix is stored in *roff format, using the man macro extensions. The special *roff formatting system has been part of Unix and many years ago was part of full-scale print-production systems. To create a man page from raw POD source, you use the `pod2man` script as shown:

```
$ pod2man script.pl
```

The formatted output is sent to STDOUT, so you will need to redirect the output. The conversion process will highlight different entities correctly. Headings, page headers and footers, and formatting will all be translated to the manual pages. The script converts the references to other manual pages so that interactive man-page readers, such as emacs, can access the linked pages correctly.

Manual pages are stored according to a series of sections that help to isolate and identify individual pages; for example, the `mkdir` command is in section 1, whereas the `mkdir` function is in section 3, sometimes 3C. The actual section names are dependent on the variety of Unix, although the major sections of 1 to 8 are unchanged on most systems.

If your POD documentation relates to a command, put it in section 1, and an extension module should be in section 3. A full list of the sections supported under System V Release 4–based Unix variants is shown in the table.

Section	Contents
1	**user commands**
1C	**basic networking commands**

Section	Contents
1F	FMLI (form and menu language interface) commands
1M	administration commands
2	system function calls
3	operating-system calls for BSD (Berkeley) Unix systems
3C	C library functions
3E	ELF executable format library functions
3G	libgen functions
3M	math functions
3N	network services functions
3S	standard I/O functions
3X	specialized libraries
4	file formats
5	miscellaneous
6	games
7	special files
8	system maintenance procedures
9	Device-Driver Interface/Driver-Kernel Interface (DDI/DDK)

Typically, the Perl-specific manual pages are installed in the man directory of the main Perl library structure. The specific location depends on the version of Perl you are using and on the platform.

37 Converting POD Files on the Fly

Pod::Html
Built-in
www.perl.com

Following the discussion of the previous number, you can use the Pod::Html module, which provides the functionality of the pod2html command, to convert files. In fact you can use the module to convert POD-based documentation on the fly through a Web server. The big benefit here is that you don't need to create the documentation beforehand or manually update the static HTML when you install a new version of the module.

The script on the CD is deceptively simple: most of the code does the work required to identify the page that has been selected. The pod2html script automatically assumes that the file you want to access is another HTML file, based on its assumption that you'll be generating static HTML pages.

You thus will need to jump through some hoops, because you have to remove and then reinsert some possible solutions until you find a matching file and then supply that information to the pod2html function to emit the HTML version of the document.

The important part really is at the top—the $root and $site_root variables hold the location of the standard and site-specific Perl library. Once the source file has been determined, all you need to do is call the pod2html function and supply the source file and root directory, and you're done. The function automatically sends the HTML to STDOUT if you don't supply a specific file in which you would normally write the information. For a sample of the output, see the following graphic.

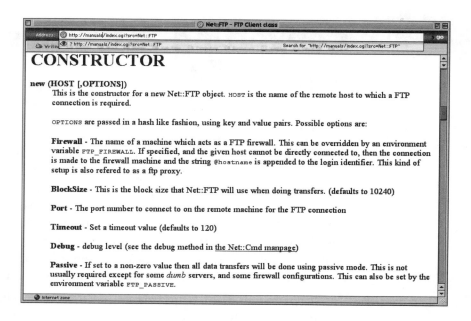

To use the script, make sure you modify the `$root` and `$site_root` variables to match your system and then install the CGI script as normal.

To view a specific page, append the following text to the URL of the CGI script:

```
?src=<MODULE>
```

`<MODULE>` is the name of the module that you want to view in HTML. For example, the following URL works on my machine to display the `Net::DNS` module documentation:

```
http://localhost/perl.cgi?src=Net::DNS
```

If you don't supply anything, the script displays the main Perl manual page, which then contains links to all the other standard Perl documents.

38 Dispatch Tables

Built-in
www.perl.com

When building a large script or application, you will occasionally want to call a particular function based on some user input. The obvious solution is to use a simple `if` statement, like so:

```
if ($command eq 'memory')
{
...
}
elsif ($command eq 'diskspace')
{
...
}
```

Although it is a perfectly acceptable solution, the coding becomes untenable when you have a large number of options. It's also relatively inefficient. Imagine if you had 10 or 15 different options—that would necessitate that many `if` statements.

Thankfully, a much easier way exists: a dispatch table. Dispatch tables are simply hashes where the keys of the hash refer to a particular command, and the corresponding values refer to the name of a function to be called. For example, the previous code can be rewritten thusly:

```
%commands = (memory => \&memory_report,
             diskspace => \&diskspace_report
             load => \&load_report );
```

Then when you receive the command from the user, check first that the command exists within the dispatch table, as follows:

```
if (exists($commands{$command}))
```

You then need to verify the existence of the corresponding function. To do so you need to resolve the function reference into a code reference, which you can then check. The code here performs the task:

```
*code = \&{$commands{$command}};
die "Function does not exist: $command"
    unless (defined(&code));
```

Actually, you can afford to skip the hash used to hold the dispatch table and instead call the dispatch functions directly. Here's code from a commercial Web-site script that accepts an "action" and "subaction" command from the browser and then builds and checks the function before calling it:

```
my $func = sprintf("%s_%s",$action,$subaction);
```

```
*code = \&{$func};
if (defined(&code))
{
    &code($user,$group,$session);
}
else
{
    display_account($user,$group,$session);
}
```

The benefits of using a dispatch table are as follows:

◆ It allows for multiple function calls based on user input without the need for a multioption if statement.

◆ You can "develop" functions and facilities into the rest of a script, even though the function may not have been created yet. You only need to supply a function definition for the script to work.

◆ You can extend and expand the script without having to manage that complex if statement.

◆ It allows debugging or audit trails to be easily compiled. Simply add the debugging or auditing code immediately before the call to the function.

I've only ever come across one downside to a dispatch table. That is, the functions you call must be supplied the same list of arguments. So you cannot change the argument list based on the function/operation name without introducing another if statement. But in a properly designed script, it is not likely to cause a problem, because you will probably supply the same information in each case—and just specify different processing. In the case of a Web script, the variables supplied by a form can be made available through a global hash.

The script on the CD provides a simple way of monitoring the three different areas of the system—the loading (including the uptime), the memory usage, and the disk space. The function selections are made dynamically based on the URL the user accesses. To add further monitoring functions, just update the HTML generated by the script and add a suitable function to handle the new command you've just introduced.

System Management

Many aspects are involved in managing the machines on your network, from the basics of monitoring them, to providing better tools and systems for managing and administering them. In this section I'll examine some of the tools available for managing your network. I'll even look at a system that controls your home!

39 Monitoring Performance

Net::MediaWeb
Martin C. Brown
www.mcslp.com

One of the most time-consuming aspects of network management is checking that the servers on your network are not overloaded or running out of swap space or disk space. I used to spend an hour or more each day checking all my machines in an effort to prevent problems or fix them before users noticed.

The time was spent even though I already had a sort of centralized but distributed system that worked as part of an Intranet. It was centralized in that there was a single point of entry into the system, but distributed in that it gleaned information from a number of servers in the network. The system, called MediaWeb, was used at an advertising agency as a way of tracking the files corresponding to individual projects.

MediaWeb stored information about the project files, and their location, both in a real-time sense—any user could get a complete list of files and where they were stored—and in a historical sense. Once a job was completed, it'd be archived to CD. But we had hundreds of CDs and no easy way to search them all.

Periodically a script would forward the list of all disc files to a central server where it would be collated. The search mechanism was through a Web browser on the Intranet, and the mechanism searched the centralized database for information.

I soon realized that I already had a tracking system that could be used to collate different types of information. I just needed to modify it to also accept other forms of information. I was already collating the files on each server; I thought, why not also collate information about the disk space? While I was at it, I monitored the memory and load information so that with a single Web page I could tell in an instant what the situation of the servers was.

The MediaWeb Theory

The way the system worked was quite simple. A central server, called the collector, periodically checked and processed the files in an "incoming" directory. How it handled each file depended on the file type, which could be determined by its name. Also stored in the name were the host from which the report was filed and the date, time, and a random number, which made up the unique ID. The server was also where the information was reported, using a series of CGI scripts that showed the current status and allowed me to view historical data.

Each client had one or more scripts that collated information about the client and then forwarded it to the central server. In order for the system to work effectively, even under extreme loads, I had to develop a system that worked in the following conditions:

◆ Data had to be collated and stored in text format, so that I could view the information even if the server (and perhaps a database on which it relied) had failed.

◆ Information had to be sent to the server over the network in as efficient and standard a way as possible. Doing so eliminated the need for a special client/server system, which in turn also made security easier.

◆ The clients had to handle server unavailability and queue information until it was available.

◆ The system had to be flexible enough to store as many different types of information as possible; this meant using simple file formats and creative use of filenames to allow the different data types to be stored and identified.

The first point was easy enough. Everything was written to a text file, and the format of the file was dependent on the data type. Mostly the format was a sequence of fields separated by colons.

The second requirement was met by using FTP. Most clients supported it, and there are FTP servers for all platforms. Supporting a directory on a server for the clients to connect and send files to was easy. I could secure it by using the usual login/password and host authentication offered within the FTP software. I could have developed my own system, but at the end of the day, files were supplied, and some of them—for example an HTTP-server log file—could be quite large. FTP is optimized for sending files.

The third point—queuing data—was handled by having a local directory store the outgoing files. When the client did successfully connect, it sent all the files in that directory. It also monitored the process (using the Net::FTP module) so that unsent files or other failures would be monitored. If the transfer failed, the files were never deleted from the queue directory, allowing them to be sent next time around.

The last point, which actually affected all the points, had more to do with the file naming than anything else. Just by giving the file a special name, I could support as many different file types as I liked. All files sent to the system were given names in the form *type.host.date.time.id*, where *type* was the type of file—for example, perf for performance data, or http for a Web log. The other fields should be obvious. Using just the file name, I could determine the file type, where it came from, and when it was created.

The Performance Monitor Scripts

The key to the plan was to use Perl to collect information from each machine. The performance client script, status.pl, got information from df, uptime, and swap (or its equivalent) and then wrote that data to a file in a special directory created in /tmp. Once the information was written out, I used Net::FTP to send the file to the collector machine. The script was run every five minutes, using cron.

At the collector end, the collector.pl script checked the incoming directory. When the script found new information, it was copied into the historical record for the host and into a separate "latest" file, used by the `ms.cgi` script.

The files were stored in a directory whose naming convention was *machine/log/date*. The *machine* is the name of the machine that the log refers to. The *log* is the type of log—perf in the case of the performance logs; http and ping (see the next number) in other instances. Note that the naming convention matches the filename of the files sent by the performance clients. The *date* is the year and month of the logged report; I appended all of the information for an entire month in one log.

The `ms.cgi` script took the latest information for each server (as stored in the latest file), and produced a summary Web page of the information. You can see a sample in the graphic. From the summary I could see the current status of the machines reporting performance data. A problem was easy to spot. I also had an e-mail alerting system, disabled in the scripts on the CD, that would warn me when the amount of disk space or swap space fell below certain levels. The scripts, like all the others, are on the CD, and they're on the Web site.

Machine Status

Filesystem	Total	Disk Used	Avail	Memory Used	Avail	Load 1mins	5mins	15min
hpux (28/08/2000, 16:00)				28.6 Mb	179.3 Mb	0.26	0.21	0.26
/	1.6 Gb	965.7 Mb	654.1 Mb					
linux (28/08/2000, 16:00)				109.8 Mb	401.7 Mb	0.00	0.00	0.00
/	460.9 Mb	324.5 Mb	136.4 Mb					
/home	1.7 Gb	366.5 Mb	1.4 Gb					
/mnt/cdrom	4.8 Mb	4.8 Mb	0 Kb					
/mnt/export	4.6 Gb	2.7 Gb	1.9 Gb					
/mnt/export/local/databases	943.1 Mb	3.5 Mb	939.6 Mb					
/mnt/export/local/http	943.1 Mb	33.0 Mb	910.0 Mb					
/mnt/export/local/vmware/nt	1.9 Gb	1.9 Gb	65.9 Mb					
/usr	943.1 Mb	490.2 Mb	452.9 Mb					
powerbook (28/08/2000, 15:00)				42.0 Mb	130.7 Mb	0.31	0.08	0.25
/	447.3 Mb	28.4 Mb	418.9 Mb					
/boot	20.0 Mb	3.5 Mb	16.5 Mb					
/home	314.3 Mb	1.5 Mb	312.7 Mb					
/mnt/cdrom	650.0 Mb	608.1 Mb	41.9 Mb					
/usr	1018.1 Mb	539.3 Mb	478.8 Mb					
twinspark (28/08/2000, 16:00)				15.7 Mb	60.8 Mb	0.14	0.05	0.04
/	101.5 Mb	55.0 Mb	46.6 Mb					
/mnt	1.7 Gb	34.0 Mb	1.6 Gb					
/opt	50.5 Mb	9 Kb	50.5 Mb					
/users	422.3 Mb	45.1 Mb	377.2 Mb					
/usr	211.4 Mb	187.0 Mb	24.4 Mb					
/usr/local	915.6 Mb	234.0 Mb	681.6 Mb					

MediaWeb is still very much a work in progress—development has to fit in between other projects. At the time of writing, MediaWeb runs on Windows, Linux, Solaris, and HP-UX machines and provides collators of log files, performance information, and the network monitor (discussed in the next number). File distribution, backup and archiving monitors, Web site log managers, and other tools are in development. See my Web site for more information and updates.

Because the system is so flexible, I can add new collators that perform all sorts of tasks. All I have to do is modify the collector so that it files the data away properly, and then write a suitable CGI script to report the information.

40 Monitoring Uptime

```
MediaWeb, Net::Ping, IO::Socket
Martin C. Brown, Built-in
www.mcwords.com
```

The problems of managing a network are multifaceted, and as you might have guessed if you've read the previous number, my own personal bugbear relates to monitoring the network. Checking if individual machines are up and how busy they are becomes a full-time job.

The scripts in this number are an extension of the MediaWeb system discussed in the last number. This time, I'm not collating information from many different machines on one machine. Instead, I'm using a single machine to check the availability of services, from the basic connectivity to Web and e-mail services.

The main script, `uptime.pl`, uses a file that defines the servers and/or services that you want to check. For each server/service available, it writes an entry into a log file. The `report.cgi` script reports on the information stored in the log files for the current month and gives an idea of the availability of the services for the current day and month.

Checking Availability

I use a combination of the `Net::Ping` and `IO::Socket` modules to check whether a particular server or service can be contacted. The core of the process is a configuration file similar to the following:

```
HEADER,Base Connectivity
IP,Internet Router,shuttle.mchome.com,
IP,NT Server,incontinent,
IP,Apple Server,atuin,
HEADER,Services
IP,Intranet Server,www.mchome.com,http
```

The `HEADER` rows are just included for clarity, and the configuration file also supports comments (using the # symbol) and blank lines. They help to group individual servers or services together. The other lines are the individual servers and services you want to check. The first field is the type of service; the script on the CD supports only IP, but I've also checked Apple-Talk and NetBIOS machines. The second field is the name as you want it to appear on reports, and the third is the actual hostname you want to check.

The last field defines the method for checking the status. If it's blank, then I use `Net::Ping` to check if I can communicate with a machine. If it holds a value, it should be the port number of the protocol you want to use to communicate with the server. For example, in the foregoing sample, I check the "Intranet Server" using `http`. I could easily use `ftp` or even `smtp` to check the status of FTP and mail servers. Irrespective of the protocol, I use `IO::Socket` to connect to the server and check if it is responding for a particular service.

Once I've got the information, I write the status information to a file that follows the same principles as the rest of the MediaWeb system. In this case the hostname, port/protocol, and year/month identify the file. For example, I might write the Intranet server status to `www.mchome.com/http/200008`. I split it by month to make it easy to get a monthly, weekly, or daily status report without the need to open multiple files.

Each entry is written as *day:time:status*, so I can pick out a particular day and time if need be, although on the whole I'm only interested in reporting on entire days or months at a time.

Of course it makes sense while I'm at it to also report the current status of the servers and services at the time the script is run so I can see at a glance which services are up without having to check the last entry in each log file. To reduce the amount of time it takes to produce the report using a CGI script, I produce a static HTML page as part of the script that can be accessed by any machine. You can see a sample in the graphic.

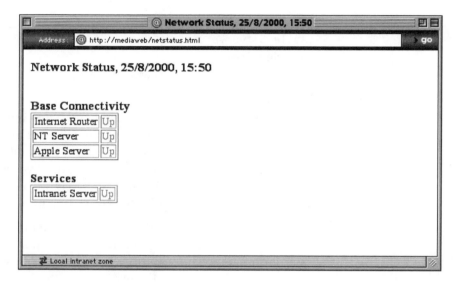

To use the script, set up the directories you want to use in the Net::MediaWeb module and then use cron to set the script to run periodically. On my home network, I use a value of 15 minutes; but you will want to set it as low as every minute on a more time-critical network. Be careful, though, as each time the script is run it uses about 10 bytes for each server/service you are checking. If you check 30 services every five minutes, you'll generate 2.5MB of information each month, so it's easy to chew through disk space. Ultimately, the system will archive and summarize the information each month, although I haven't quite gotten that far yet!

Reporting the Status

To report the information is quite easy—all you have to do is open up this month's file and count up the number of successful and unsuccessful attempts. Because the information is stored in a file that contains the entire month, you can get not only a daily, but also a weekly and monthly, report of the uptime of the different services.

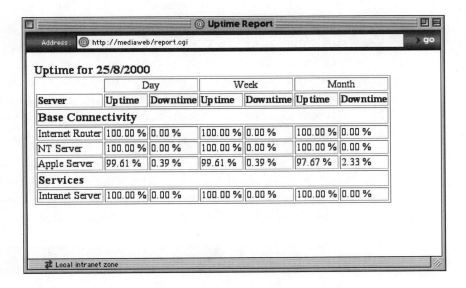

41 Communicating with Syslog

Sys::Syslog
Built-in
www.perl.com

You will occasionally want a script or application that reports errors to log the problems into a central log file, rather than simply write the error to STDERR or produce your own personal log file. Many different ways exist of doing this, but the most practical on Unix systems is to talk to the syslog daemon and give it your error message.

The syslog system works with a basic combination of a series of logging options and a facility or area in which to record the entry. The normal operation is for the syslog system to take the error message and write it to the system log. Depending on the severity of the error, it may also write the information directly to the console and if necessary will even send an e-mail to the systems administrator.

Perl comes with the Sys::Syslog module that provides a very simple interface for reporting information to the syslog system; the information is in turn written to the system logs, often held at /var/log/syslog or similar. The best way to use the system if you intend to log information in this way is to call the openlog function at the start of your script, like so:

```
openlog($myprog, 'cons,pid', 'user')
```

The first argument is the identity of the program. The string is attached to the beginning of each message within the log. The second argument defines the options used when writing to the log, as a comma-separated list of words. The available options are shown in the table.

Option	Description
pid	**Includes the process ID with the message.**
ndelay	**Opens the connection to the** syslog **system immediately, rather than waiting until the first message is reported.**
cons	**Sends the error directly to the console if the log cannot be written.**
nowait	**Does not wait for children to log messages on the console. The option should be used by processes that enable notification of child termination via** $SIG{CLD}, **because** syslog **might otherwise block while waiting for a child whose exit status has already been collected.**

The last argument defines the facility in which the error occurred. Again, the facilities are system dependent, but the corresponding table lists some likely candidates.

Facility	Description
authpriv	**security/authorization messages**
cron	**scheduling (**cron **and** at**)**

Facility	Description
daemon	**other system daemons**
kern	**kernel messages**
lpr	**line-printer subsystem**
mail	**mail subsystem**
news	**USENET news subsystem**
syslog	**messages generated internally by** syslogd
user	**generic user-level messages**
uucp	**UUCP subsystem level**

To report an error, you make a call to the syslog function. The function uses the options specified when the log was opened, in addition to the arguments you supply to syslog (). Consider the following line:

```
syslog('debug',"Got the error %m from %s", $function);
```

The first argument is the priority of the message. The syslog system is configured through the syslog.conf file that determines what the syslog daemon does when a message is sent to the system. Priorities supported by the Perl module are listed in the table.

Priority	Description
emerg	**Facility is unusable.**
alert	**Action must be taken immediately.**
crit	**Critical conditions.**
err	**Error conditions.**
warning	**Warning conditions.**
notice	**Normal, but significant, condition.**

Priority	Description
info	**Informational message.**
debug	**Debug-level message.**

The second argument is a format, as used by `printf`, that supplies the message; any remaining arguments are applied to the corresponding elements in the format. The only difference is that the format string %m is replaced with the string value of $!.

Once you've finished writing to the log, use the `closelog` function to close the connection. The following code is a complete example:

```
use Sys::Syslog;

openlog('perl', 'cons,pid', 'user');
syslog('warning' ,'Something happened');
closelog();
```

It produces the following entry on a Solaris system:

```
Jul 19 11:13:57 twinspark perl[2686]: Something happened
```

There are two scripts on the CD. One simply logs any message to the `syslog` system. The other should be run periodically by `cron` to log uptime and memory information to the system log so that you can trace any problems and errors.

To use the first script, you need to supply at least four arguments on the command line. The first three are the option, facility, and priority information, and the fourth and any remaining argument are separated by spaces and inserted as the message. The following is an example:

```
$ syslog.pl cons user warning Changed /etc/passwd
```

For the second script, you need to create an entry in the `root crontab`, as shown:

```
0,15,30,45 * * * * slstat.pl
```

The code will place the `uptime` and swap information into the `syslog` as an informational entry every 15 minutes. I use the code as a way of identifying problems after a machine crashes or begins to slow down. By getting a quick idea of the load and memory usage, you can often isolate and identify problems. The scripts should work on Linux, Solaris, and HP-UX. Of course, a better system is probably to use MediaWeb!

42 Reading and Writing Tar Archives

Archive::Tar, File::Find
Stephen Zander
www.cpan.org

I've been frustrated over the years about the transferal of Web sites from my local machine to my hosting service. I have copies of all my Web sites on one of my Linux servers, and it's here that I make changes and updates. But moving the sites to the hosting service is unnecessarily complex.

Although I could code the following, which backs up any files or directories that have changed in the last seven days, it doesn't quite do what I want:

```
$ find . -mtime -7 -print|xargs tar cf update.tar
```

For a start, many of the sites are also tracked using CVS, and I don't want to transfer the CVS information files along with the site. They just take up space. Furthermore, I don't want to transfer many other files—for example, the backup files generated by emacs and temporary files created as I update the site.

I could write a shell script to delete those files or temporarily move them to create a better list of files to add to the archive. However, a shell script is still needed, and I'll be limited as to the number of files I can supply to tar on the command line to add to the archive file.

Perl provides two solutions to the problem. The first is the File::Find module, which you can use to find and select the files you want. The other module is Archive::Tar, which provides a method within Perl for writing tar files directly.

Using File::Find

The File::Find module is part of the standard Perl library and provides a method for traversing an entire directory tree and examining each file. The module works with two components—a function that traverses the tree and a function you supply that processes and selects each file.

NOTE If you want the full, rather than relative, pathname to the file or directory, use $File::Find::name.

For example, the following script prints out files (not directories) modified in the last seven days:

```perl
use File::Find;
&find(\&wanted,'.');

exit;
sub wanted
{
    (($dev,$ino,$mode,$nlink,$uid,$gid) = lstat($_)) &&
    (int(-M _) < 7) &&
    -f _ or return;
    print "$_\n";
}
```

For each file or directory in the tree that's found, the name is placed into $_, and the wanted function is called. It's up to you to do what you like with the file.

NOTE If you want a quick way of producing a File::Find-based script that selects individual files, try using find2Perl. It accepts the same command-line arguments that the Unix find command does. Program it like so:

```
$ find2Perl -mtime 7 -type f >myfind.pl
```

Using Archive::Tar

The `Archive::Tar` module is even easier to use than `File::Find`. Follow the simple steps:

1. Create a new archive object.

2. Supply a list of the files you want added to the archive.

3. Write out the archive!

In fact, you can even code it in only three lines:

```
my $archive = Archive::Tar->new();
$archive->add_files(@filelist);
$archive->write($arcname,1);
```

The important method is `write`–the first argument is the name you want to give to the file, and the second argument is a simple Boolean value. If the Boolean value is true, then the archive will be compressed using the `Gzip` Unix program.

Putting the Functions Together

To bond the two functions, simply append each file that you want in the archive into an array and then supply that array as the list of files to add to the archive. The previous three-line fragment of code comes from the script on the CD. It selects all files that don't start with a period, are `emacs` backup files, or have the string "CVS" in their path.

The script also uses a base file that is updated each time the script is called and is used as a reference point for the modification time on each file. So each time the script is called, the modification time of the files in the directory is compared against the file. If the file is more recent, then it's added to the list of files you'll write to the archive.

To use the script, supply the base archive name (the date and time of creation will be added) and the name of the comparison file to use, followed by the list of directories you want to search for matching files. For example, consider the following:

```
$ archive.pl update .lastarchive .
Adding ./index.shtml to archive
```

```
Adding ./translate.pl to archive
Adding ./ssi/topbar.html to archive
Adding ./ssi/panel/gen/update to archive
...
Adding ./about/people.shtml to archive
Writing 118 files to update.20000828.1348.tar.gz
```

The command will create a tar archive called
updates.20000828.1348.tar.gz, containing all the files newer than
.lastarchive, from the files and directories in the current directory.

43 Using Perl to Control Your Home

MisterHouse
Bruce Winter
www.misterhouse.net

Many of you have seen the films from the '50s and '60s heralding the new age of automated homes, with promises of equipment that would do everything for you, from automatically ironing your clothes, through putting on coffee and shutting curtains. These films promised an unbelievable amount of automation, enabling all to enjoy more free time.

Some predictions came true—automatic coffee machines are a reality, but no machines automatically iron clothes. Even in the '80s people were promised the ability to call home and ask the house to switch on the heating, run a bath, and make dinner. Whereas some of the predictions have come true, the technology is still a long way from the Star Trek–inspired automation.

But you can automate some tasks in the home with a system called X10. The system uses a combination of two technologies in order to produce the desired effect. The first is the use of small boxes that provide a means of controlling other devices. You can tell a single box to switch on a lamp, for example, or to change the channel on your TV.

Within a single room, it wouldn't be much use. The room would have to be very large for you not to get up and turn on the light, and you probably already have a remote-control TV. You need a way to communicate with these devices in other rooms—in other words, some kind of network.

Many people are now beginning to experience the benefits of networking in their home. People who have more than one computer need to communicate between them, and the explosion in users working from home means that large numbers of people now have a computer for each family member and need to communicate both internally and externally with each other.

The use of small boxes sounds ideal—put all the little boxes on a wired network and you've got complete control. The problem is, fitting any home-networking system is a difficult, messy, and sometimes-destructive process. This is where the second technology comes in. Although you may not know it, your house already has a built-in network you can use—your power cables.

When your home was built, the power sockets were connected, probably in a ring formation, and all of them end up at the same connection terminal at the fuse box in your house. The X10 system leverages the cabling used to supply power as a method of communication. You don't need very fast speeds; a single instruction to tell a lamp to turn on is not very data intensive!

You can see a sample of the system in the graphic—the computer is connected to an X10 communication box to provide a connection to the X10 system. The X10 box is connected to the power socket, which in turn is connected through the ring to the TV and lamp. When you want to turn on the lamp, you tell the X10 system, and it sends the instruction over the power cable to the control box for the lamp, which in turn turns on the power.

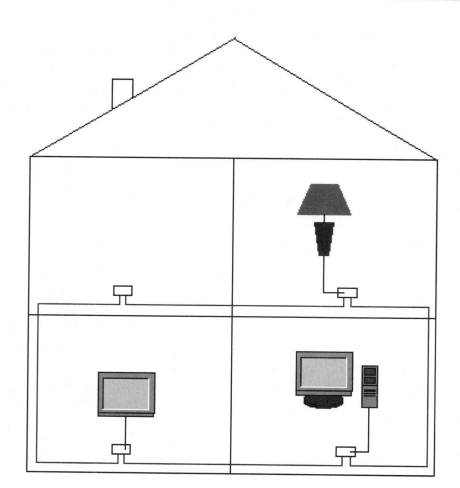

In order for the system to work, each X10 appliance must have a unique number, and you need some form of controller—most homes will use a computer, but you can also use an infrared control to communicate with the other X10 devices.

Simple!

The same process works for the TV if you get a suitable two-way infrared adapter. You could be upstairs on the computer and tell the TV to turn on so it is ready for you when you get downstairs. Even better, you can set up macros that do a number of tasks—you might have a "movie" macro that dims the lights, closes the curtains, turns on the TV and DVD player, and starts the popcorn maker in the kitchen!

MisterHouse

Although a remote control provides the most obvious (and portable!) solution, it's not ideal if you want to have more complex controls and macros, timing systems, and more remote (i.e., out of the house) control of your home.

A computer-based connection stands out here. You can control the X10 system using a simple serial interface and an X10 interface controller.

Although modules available from CPAN allow you to communicate with an X10 controller through your serial port, by far the most complete solution is MisterHouse. Written by Bruce Winter, an IBM engineer, it allows you to develop an interface that works with both Tk and a Web browser to control your home. You can even use a combination of speech recognition and text-to-speech interfaces to control and interact with your X10 system.

You can see a sample Web interface and the Tk interface in the following two graphics.

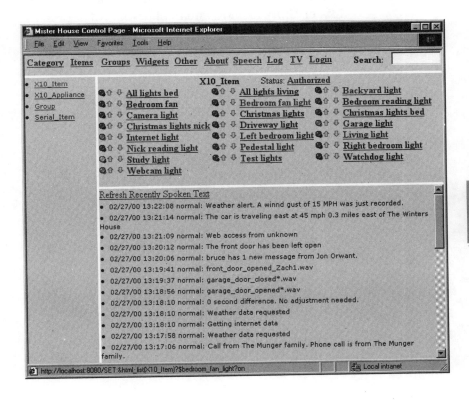

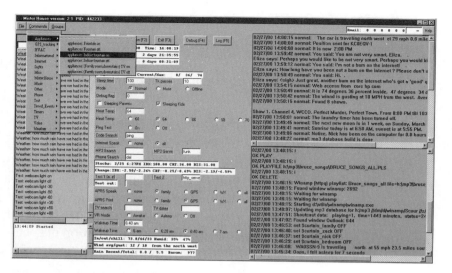

You can see from the graphics that the information and control available to you is extensive. You can even integrate your MP3 audio library with MisterHouse to allow you to play your MP3s both in specific rooms and through other rooms throughout the house. The next graphic shows the MP3 control interface for MP3 jukeboxes.

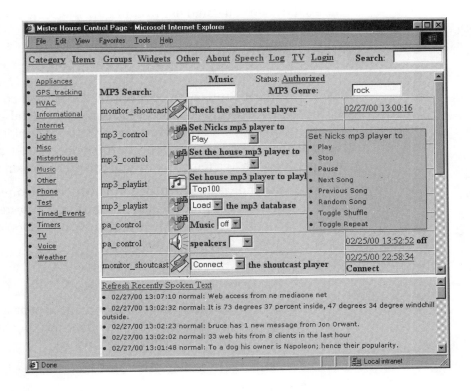

Using MisterHouse

Configuring MisterHouse is very simple—the software is included on the CD. You'll need Perl under Linux/Unix or ActivePerl under Windows. You'll also need some extensions that allow communication with the X10 system and the Tk GUI interface module. You'll also need to install the Microsoft voice extensions or, under Unix, the ViaVoice application, if you want to communicate with the system using voice commands.

Alternatively, you can avoid the whole Perl issue and download a standalone binary containing the core MisterHouse code. The configuration of the system uses a number of external files, all of which are written using Perl.

Here's the code you could use to configure the dishwasher to come on at a specific time:

```
$dishwasher = new X10_Item 'B1';
set $dishwasher ON if time_now '10:30 PM';
```

The 'B1' is the identification code for the dishwasher controller. You can see here that I've written a time-based entry. You can also key on external events supplied by some of the two-way X10 interfaces. These can be analog or digital, so you can get simple on/off details as well as more complex information such as a temperature and weather from suitable equipment.

The following code is for playing a sound when someone triggers a movement sensor—X10 supports most of the basic alarm systems, such as PIR (Passive Infrared, the infrared heat and motion sensors) and make-or-break contacts for doors and windows:

```
play(file => 'stairs_creek*.wav')
    if state_now $movement_sensor eq ON;
```

Finally, the voice interface can be configured to accept specific words as control statements. For example, the result of speaking the phrase "open the bedroom curtains" should be pretty obvious:

```
$v_bedroom_curtain = new Voice_Cmd '[open,close] the bedroom
curtains';
curtain_on('bedroom', $state) if $state = said
$v_bedroom_curtain;
```

Pretty cool.

Platform Specialties

Despite its Unix roots, Perl is not a Unix-only language. Excellent tools and extensions are available for all sorts of platforms; in this section I'm going to look at how to use some of the Mac and Windows tools. Did you know that it's possible to control another application from within Perl?

44 Communicating with AppleScript

```
MacPerl::DoAppleScript
```
Matthias Neeracher
`www.iis.ee.ethz.ch/~neeri/macintosh/perl.html`

Most operating systems have some form of scripting ability. Unix is probably the most naturally powerful because most Unix flavors come with shells, awk, and other utilities like sed, cut, and grep that can be bonded together to produce quite complex tools. Most Linux and BSD distributions even come with Perl!

Windows comes with batch files and the Windows Scripting Host, a generic scripting system that can also be expanded with other languages, including Visual Basic (in its VBScript form) and Perl.

The odd one out, though, is the MacOS. Because it doesn't have any natural-text interface, producing a scriptable language is more difficult. Although some scriptable solutions have appeared over the years, such as tools like Now Utilities and KeyQuencer, it wasn't until System 7.5 that Apple introduced their own script system—AppleScript.

AppleScript works in a similar fashion to most of the other scripting languages, including Perl. The main difference is that because Mac applications aren't command line in nature, you actually "tell" an application to perform a particular task, and it's up to the application to know what it is you're doing. The communication is two way, which means you can not only write an AppleScript straight off, but you can also "record" what you do into a new AppleScript.

Talking to AppleScript

From within Perl you can use the `MacPerl::DoAppleScript` function to execute an arbitrary AppleScript script. For example, you could empty the trash from within a Perl script by using the following lines:

```
MacPerl::DoAppleScript(<<EOF);
tell application "Finder"
    activate
    empty trash
end tell
EOF
```

Because AppleScript talks directly to applications, you can also get Apple-Script to talk to another language that's been embedded into an application. For example, the following, from within Perl, will tell Word to print the current document:

```
MacPerl::DoAppleScript(<<EOF);
tell application "Microsoft Word"
activate
do Visual Basic "Application.PrintOut FileName:=\"\",
Range:=wdPrintRangeOfPages, Item:= _
wdPrintDocumentContent, Copies:=1, Pages:=\"1-32000\", Page-
Type:= _
wdPrintAllPages, Collate:=True, Background:=False"
end tell
EOF
```

What the code does is talk to Microsoft Word and tell the Visual Basic for Applications language built into Word to print the document. I actually recorded the foregoing code using `ScriptEditor` and then just embedded the AppleScript document into a Perl document—it really is that easy!

Replying to AppleScript

The MacPerl::Reply function sends a response back to an AppleScript script from MacPerl. So you can, from AppleScript, ask MacPerl to perform a task and then get a response from MacPerl about the success or return value.

For example, here's an AppleScript script that tells MacPerl to send back the string "Hello World," which I just display in a dialog box:

```
tell application "MacPerl"
    activate
    make new document
    set Spot 1 of document 1 to "MacPerl::Reply('Hello World');
    "
    set reply to Do Script "MacPerl::Reply('Hello World');
" directory file "Sulaco:Applications:MacPerl ƒ:"
    display dialog reply with icon caution buttons {"OK"}
default button 1
    end tell
```

The code listed here is fairly simplistic, but without going into detail about AppleScript—which is not what this book is about—it's difficult to get more detailed input. If you can get AppleScript to talk to MacPerl, you can do anything that MacPerl does, and with some work you can easily get MacPerl to return information back to a calling AppleScript script.

45 Developing a MacOS Interface

MacPerl
Matthias Neeracher
www.iis.ee.ethz.ch/~neeri/macintosh/perl.html

Although I'm a fairly big user and fan of the MacPerl distribution, it has one small failing that often prevents me from using it as a development platform. I nearly always resort to using some form of Unix, and MacPerl does not support, or include any sort of provision for, the Tk interface system.

That problem, coupled with the obvious lack of a command-line interface, can often make developing a MacPerl-based application very difficult.

But you're saved, as Matthias Neeracher has produced a series of functions that support a set of dialog boxes using the standard MacOS interface toolkit. So you can develop a professional-looking MacPerl-based application without the need for Tk (which doesn't look like a genuine MacOS application anyway).

Answer

The most basic of Neeracher's functions is Answer, which displays a dialog box to the user, in the same fashion as a warning dialog. You get a prompt and the ability to display up to three buttons. The last button is always the default. For example, the following code fragment presents a dialog with the message "Delete File" and two buttons:

```
MacPerl::Answer("Delete File","OK","Cancel");
```

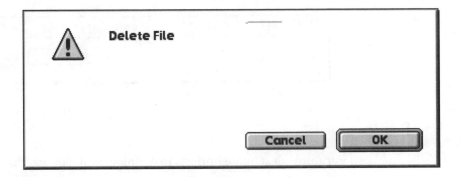

The function's return value is a number relating to the button that was pressed, starting at zero for the first button. So from the example given, a "0" would be returned if "OK" were clicked and "1" if "Cancel" were clicked. If you want to support more than three buttons, then you will need to use the Pick function (discussed later in this number).

Ask

The Ask function is slightly more interactive than Answer—it presents a dialog box into which the user can type a response. You would use the function like so:

```
$name = MacPerl::Ask('Enter your name');
```

You can also supply a default value, which will be preentered into the field (and can obviously be overwritten) by specifying a second argument. Write the code like the following:

```
$name = MacPerl::Ask('Enter your name', 'Martin');
```

The graphic shows a dialog box presented by the Ask function. The value entered is returned by the function, or "undef" is returned if the Cancel button is clicked.

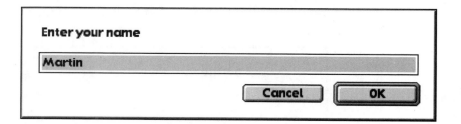

Pick

For multiple-choice options in a dialog, you can use the Pick function. It provides a list of options and two buttons, "OK" and "Cancel." The first argument is the prompt, which becomes the title of the window, and the remaining arguments become the values for the list. The function returns the string selected as the value. For example, the function call shown produces a dialog box like the one in the graphic:

```
MacPerl::Pick("Pick a colour", "Blue",
              "Green", "Red", "Yellow");
```

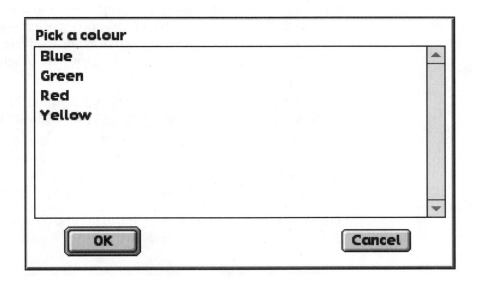

Choose

The Choose function is a complex function that provides a unified interface to finding different types of resources on the network. The term "network" sounds restrictive. In fact the Choose function produces a standard selection dialog for files, network servers, and printers. The most popular use of the function is for selecting a file or directory within a script.

The interface is controlled through the use of a special DOMAIN argument, the first argument supplied to the function. DOMAIN defines the type of resource search, for example for a file, directory, or network server. You may use many different types and combinations of arguments. The following is an example:

```
MacPerl::Choose(DOMAIN, TYPE, PROMPT [,
                CONSTRAINT [, FLAGS [, DEFAULT]]])
```

The function requires support from the GUSI.ph library, which, among other tasks, supplies the packing and unpacking routines used for different arguments.

To use the file domain, which allows you to present a standard file-selection dialog, use the AF_FILE constant. The result is a modal dialog box (which means that it's the only active window—you cannot switch to another application or window), allowing the user to select a file (or directory) from a list.

For example, the code fragment here pops up a normal file-selection dialog box, allowing you to select only files with a *TYPE* code of "TEXT":

```
require "GUSI.ph";

$file = MacPerl::Choose(&GUSI::AF_FILE, 0, "",
                    &GUSI::pack_sa_constr_file("TEXT", ""));
```

It presents you with a dialog box similar to the one shown. The return value will be the full path to the file selected.

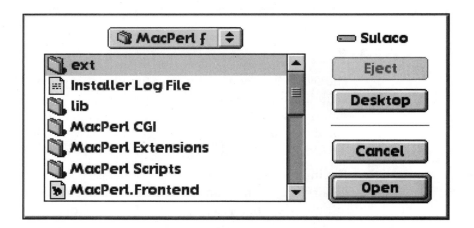

To provide a dialog box for selecting a directory rather than a file, write code like so:

```
require "GUSI.ph";

$dir = MacPerl::Choose(&GUSI::AF_FILE, 0,
                    "", "", &GUSI::CHOOSE_DIR);
```

The dialog box displayed is shown.

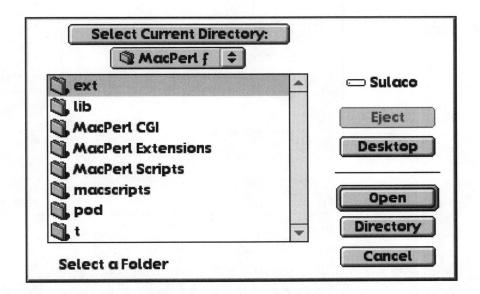

To present a dialog box that allows you to select a new file (and therefore enter a file name), write the code like so:

```
require "GUSI.ph";

$file = MacPerl::Choose(&GUSI::AF_FILE, 0, "", "",
            &GUSI::CHOOSE_NEW + &GUSI::CHOOSE_DEFAULT,
                "source.txt");
```

The snippet displays a dialog box as shown, with the name of the file chosen by default highlighted.

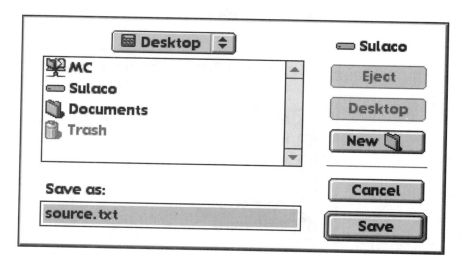

46 Checking Windows NT Performance

Win32::PerfLib
Jutta M. Klebe
www.bybyte.de/jmk

Back in number 38, I looked at a script that monitored the performance of Unix machines. Although a Windows version of the script exists, it reports disk and memory information but completely ignores the equivalent of the Unix uptime command. Nothing on the Windows side of the fence is so straightforward as a "load" counter. Windows NT (and 2000) tracks and records hundreds of different system indicators. Performing a count on a typical Windows 2000 machine returns no less than 1,842 different counters.

The counters record everything from the number of generic packets sent and received to the number of specific packet types received. You can even get a count of the number of files installed on a machine.

The `Win32::PerfLib` module provides the necessary functions and methods for accessing the information stored within the counters and the functions for resolving the counter names and IDs. Windows NT and 2000 have their own performance-monitoring tools to show you the information that can be obtained from the counters. The Windows 2000 tool, for example, is called `Performance`. The names of the tools used here are identical to those you can use with `Win32::PerfLib`.

Getting Counter Names

The `Win32::PerfLib::GetCounterNames` function places the numerical IDs and counter names into the keys and values of a hash. For example, the following code will place the information into the `%counters` hash:

```
Win32::PerfLib::GetCounterNames('',\%counters);
```

The first argument is the name of the machine you want to get the counters from. Like other parts of Windows NT and 2000, you can get the information from a remote machine, assuming you have the right privileges.

Because the information is returned as IDs related to counter names, you'll probably want to create an inverse hash so you can get counter IDs based on their names. For that, use something like:

```
%r_counter = map { $counter{$_} => $_ } keys %counter;
```

The Object Structure

The `Win32::PerfLib` module uses an object-based interface for getting information. The main object created has a very complex structure that I won't cover in minute detail. However, I will cover the basic structure here.

The base object structure looks like the following:

```
$hashref = {'NumObjectTypes'    => VALUE
            'Objects'           => HASHREF
            'PerfFreq'          => VALUE
            'PerfTime'          => VALUE
            'PerfTime100nSec'   => VALUE
            'SystemName'        => STRING
            'SystemTime'        => VALUE
           };
```

Most of the key/value pair combinations should be obvious. For example, the 'PerfFreq' entry gives the period between individual logs of the counter. The interesting entry is the 'Objects' key—it contains a hash that in turn contains the individual counter records.

The hash objects look like so:

```
$hashref->{Objects}->{<object1>} = {
        'DetailLevel'           => VALUE
        'Instances'             => HASHREF
        'Counters'              => HASHREF
        'NumCounters'           => VALUE
        'NumInstances'          => VALUE
        'ObjectHelpTitleIndex'  => VALUE
        'ObjectNameTitleIndex'  => VALUE
        'PerfFreq'              => VALUE
        'PerfTime'              => VALUE
    };
```

Again, it's the 'Instances' and 'Counters' keys that contain a hash with useful information. An Instance is an instance of a series of value counts and contains a hash reference to a load of counter objects. The counter object, whether accessed at the present level or as part of an instance record, looks like the following:

```
$hashref->{Objects}->{<object1>}->{Instances}->{<1>}-
>{Counters}->{<1>} = {
    Counter                 => VALUE
    CounterHelpTitleIndex   => VALUE
    CounterNameTitleIndex   => VALUE
```

```
        CounterSize          => VALUE
        CounterType          => VALUE
        DefaultScale         => VALUE
        DetailLevel          => VALUE
        Display              => STRING
    }
```

Finally, you're at the level where you can start to get some information. The `Counter` is the information you want; everything else tells you about the information and how should it be displayed.

The script on the CD gets the system uptime—that is, the number of days, hours, minutes, and seconds since the machine was started.

47 Talking to Microsoft Word

`Win32::OLE`
Gurusamy Sarathay, Jan Dubois
`www.activestate.com`

As a programmer, I find many aspects of Perl cool. Over the years I've created some wonderful things with Perl with great ease; considering Perl's style and relative grace, it's hard to find something new and exciting to make me stay up all night and simply play.

But it happened relatively recently with ActiveState's version of Perl for Windows and the `Win32::OLE` module, a standard part of the ActivePerl distribution from ActiveState. The module provides an interface to the OLE (Object Linking and Embedding) system on Windows machines. It's the OLE system that allows you to share and use COM (Common Object Method) objects. Without going into too much detail, the OLE/COM system allows you to communicate with other Windows applications by using them as objects.

For example, I can open a Word document and then access the different elements of that document through an object-oriented interface. For a writer the option opens up a lot of possibilities. Before sending in a chapter or finalizing a book, I'll often take out samples or sections of the book and analyze them in different ways. I might extract all the text and identify all keywords or phrases that I used so I can be sure I've been consistent. For programming books I might pick out all of the snippets of code and run them through Perl to ensure that the code works.

Traditionally I might have done so by saving as text and either manually extracting the elements or using a macro to delete all but the text I wanted to keep. The procedure is neither practical nor very efficient for a 1,200-page book!

Instead, I can use a Perl script and the `Win32::OLE` interface to do it for me. More than that, once the information has been extracted I can do what I like with it.

Opening a COM object

The system works because many applications—especially those created by Microsoft applications—use and store different components of a document in an object format. For example, a document in Word is split into paragraphs, and each paragraph contains information such as the paragraph style and formatting, tab stops, whether it has a drop cap, and of course the raw text.

The Windows system allows you to open a COM object—which is what a Word document is—and then access the individual components. To open an existing object, you simply supply the name of the file you want to open, like so:

```
use Win32::OLE;

$document = Win32::OLE->GetObject('letter.doc');
```

Alternatively, to create a new object, just supply the OLE class when creating it. For example, to create a Word document, the code would be:

```
$document = new Win32::OLE('Word.Document');
```

N O T E You can find a list of suitable OLE classes using the System Information utility, which can be found in the System Tools folder in the Accessories Folder in the Start menu.

In both cases, the resulting scalar variable contains a reference to the appropriate object. It is not a Perl object (although it behaves like one)—the Win32::OLE module just provides an interface to the underlying COM object.

COM Object Manipulation

You can manipulate a COM object using the normal method and attribute calls available in Perl. For example, you can automatically open and print a file using the following code:

```
use Win32::OLE;
$document = Win32::OLE->GetObject('letter.doc');
if ($document)
{
    $application = $document->{Parent};
    $application->{Visible} = 1;
    $application->PrintOut();
    $application->Quit();
}
```

First you get a reference to the parent object—in this case the Word application. Then you make sure it's visible. Otherwise you won't see the dialogs. Then tell it to print the active document.

Script Samples

Two scripts are included on the CD, both of which I use when writing. The first, docinfo.pl, extracts the document properties for a given Word document. I use the number of lines in a document as a way of tracking my progress, so using this script I can get that information without having to manually open each file. Properties are available via a method off the top-level document object.

The second, `extract.pl`, extracts paragraphs from a given file that match the "Code Listing" style, the one used for inline source code. The resulting paragraphs are each written to their files. The script works using the `Paragraphs` method, which returns a list of paragraph objects. You can then work through each paragraph and access its `Style` property, which contains the style's name.

48 Talking to Microsoft Excel

```
Win32::OLE
```
Gurusamy Sarathay, Jan Dubois
`www.activestate.com`

I've already taken a quick look at interfacing to the OLE system that supports the object system employed by Windows and ergo Microsoft Office. For Word the structure is quite complex. A document is split into a number of high-level elements, including tables of contents, indexes, embedded pictures, and finally the information that everybody is really interested in, the paragraphs that actually make up the document. The complex model adds extra levels of complication to what seems relatively easy when you simply open a document within Word.

By comparison, the layout for an Excel document is significantly simpler, both from a visual and programming perspective. Although some top-level elements seem unrelated to the spreadsheet component of an Excel document, the spreadsheet itself is easy to understand.

The basic layout of an Excel document can be seen in the graphic. You can see that it's made up from a series of worksheets, and each worksheet is subdivided into a series of ranges and/or cells, with each range referring to a selection of cells. The ranges are not hard coded—you could create a range with only a single cell, or one with an entire range of cells.

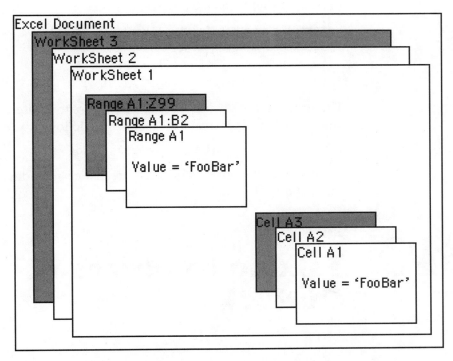

So you could, for example, update an individual cell like so:

```
$range = $worksheet->Range('A1');
$range->{Value} = "Test Cell Contents";
```

Or you could update a range of values if you supply the object with a reference to an array, as shown:

```
$range = $worksheet->Range('A1:C1');
$range->{Value} = ['Filename', 'Size', 'Time'];
```

The sequence for accessing a range of cells as shown here follows the layout of the diagram. Assuming you start with an application object, the sequence is:

1. Create/Open Excel Application Object

2. Open an Excel Workbook

3. Open a Worksheet within a Workbook

4. Open a Range within a Worksheet

In code it would take the following form:

```
$excel = new Win32::OLE('Excel.Application');
$workbook = $excel->Workbooks->Add();
$worksheet = $workbook->Worksheets(1);
$range = $worksheet->Range('A1:C1');
```

The script on the CD uses the sequence here to create a directory listing within an Excel spreadsheet. Consider the following example:

```
C:\> perl excel.pl Documents.xls *.doc
```

The resulting Documents.xls Excel spreadsheet includes a list of names, file sizes, and the last modification time.

49 Talking to Microsoft Outlook

```
Win32::OLE
```
Gurusamy Sarathay, Jan Dubois
www.activestate.com

For my last look at Win32::OLE, I'm going to send a message from a Windows machine using Microsoft Outlook. Sending e-mail is actually one of the most common queries about using Perl under Windows.

Under Unix the most common way is to use open to create a pipe to the sendmail utility, and then supply the message destination, sender, and body. Under Windows there is no sendmail, and although many utilities have sprouted up over the years for emulating the functionality of sendmail, they still don't address one of the most useful aspects of the sendmail system.

When you send a message using sendmail on a Unix box, the message is put into a queue of messages to be sent. Most of the time, sendmail will have been configured so that it automatically sends it on to the next machine in the chain that accepts e-mail for that user. Because the e-mail sits in the queue, you don't need to have a permanent connection to the Internet— sendmail will send the message the next time you're connected.

Most of the simple sendmail implementations available on Windows just resend the message on to an SMTP mail server, and effectively lose the message if the destination can't be reached.

Of course, you could use the Net::SMTP module from Graham Barr to talk directly to an SMTP mail server. But wait—you would have the same problem again. You'd still rely on having an SMTP server to talk to. Furthermore, even if you configure Perl to talk to the SMTP server supported by your ISP, your Windows machine probably won't dial in to your ISP for you.

If you don't have a local SMTP server to talk to, you've got a problem. You could use a proper mail server, like VPOP or PostOffice, or even Microsoft Exchange. Most of the time, though, such applications are overkill.

The solution is to use Win32::OLE to talk to Microsoft Outlook, which would send the message. Like the previous Word and Excel samples, the process is incredibly simple. In fact it can be resolved down to just six lines! Look:

```
$outlook = new Win32::OLE('Outlook.Application');
$mailitem = $outlook->CreateItem(olMailItem);
$mailitem->{To} = $to;
$mailitem->{Subject} = $subject;
$mailitem->{Body} = $body;
$mailitem->Send();
```

The final line is the one you're interested in. The Send method places the e-mail into Outlook's Outgoing folder, which means that it will only be sent when you either tell Outlook to send the mail, or the periodic send operation occurs. So the message will be queued and sent along with all your other mail.

Better still, if you're using a dial-up connection, Outlook knows how to tell the dial-up system to dial in to and connect to your ISP. With the combination of queuing and dial-up awareness, you can be guaranteed that the mail will be sent correctly, whether or not you happen to be connected to your ISP at the time the e-mail is created.

The script on the CD will allow you to send an e-mail from the command line, using Perl to talk to Outlook. The command looks like so:

```
C:\>perl sendmail.pl mc@mcwords.com
Subject: Testing
Message:
Hello, this is a test message

Message queued
```

Like Excel and Word, the OLE system provides much more than the ability to send e-mail. Anything you can do with Visual Basic and the macro system can be done with Perl and the Win32::OLE module.

50 Windows NT Service Management

```
Win32::Service
Gurusamy Sarathay
www.activestate.com
```

One of the lesser-known features in Windows NT is its network-level operation. It sounds obvious, but in fact most people don't really understand that NT is a network operating system. The network interoperability is transparent; most people, then, consider the extent of NT's abilities as only having to use a single password to log in to an NT network.

In fact, provided you have suitable Administrator privileges, you can perform a wide range of tasks remotely over the network, from adding users to controlling the services that provide file sharing, printer sharing, and similar background processes. Through a series of extensions for Perl, you can control certain aspects of NT over the network. The extensions show how versatile Perl can be for solving a whole range of problems.

In essence a Windows NT service is just a background process that's designed to look after a specific task. For example, different services exist for file and printer sharing, web serving, NNTP/SMTP services, and so on. The service system also provides some of the basic functionality required by the machine. A "Plug and Play" service, for instance, manages the interface between the hardware and the plug-and-play device drivers.

Using Perl, you can call the `Win32::Service` module to control services on a Windows NT or Windows 2000 machine. The interface is very simple, with functions for listing, starting, stopping, and getting the status of the different services on a machine. In order to control services, though, you'll need administrator privileges on the machine in question.

The Win32::Service Module

The `Win32::Service` module supports six functions, which are detailed in the first table. All services have two names—the long name used to display the service in the Services control panel, and a shorter name used to identify the service internally. In all cases you must use the short name when starting, stopping, or getting the status of a service.

Function	Description
GetServices(*HOST*, *SERVICES*)	**Gets the list of services from** *HOST* **and places the information into the hash pointed to by** *SERVICES*. **The keys contain the long service names and the values of the short. If no value (an empty string) is supplied for** *HOST*, **then the local machine is used instead.**
StartService(*HOST*, *SERVICE*)	**Starts the** *SERVICE*, **as identified by its short name, on** *HOST*.
StopService(*HOST*, *SERVICE*)	**Stops the** *SERVICE*, **as identified by its short name, on** *HOST*.
PauseService(*HOST*, *SERVICE*)	**Pauses the** *SERVICE*, **as identified by its short name, on** *HOST*.
ResumeService(*HOST*, *SERVICE*)	**Resumes the** *SERVICE*, **as identified by its short name, on** *HOST*.

Function	Description
GetStatus(*HOST*, *SERVICE*, *STATUS*)	**Places the current status information for** *SERVICE* **on** *HOST* **into the hash pointed to by** *STATUS*. **See the next table for details of the keys and values in the hash.**

The next table describes the hash keys for a given service.

Key	Description
ServiceType	**The type of service, supplied as a numerical constant. Values start at zero and are, in order, Win32 Owner process, Win32 Shared process, Kernel driver, File System driver.**
CurrentState	**The status of the service supplied as a numerical value. See the next table for details on the possible values and their meaning.**
ControlsAccepted	**The list of control codes accepted by the command.**
Win32ExitCode	**The generic error code returned when the service starts or stops.**
ServiceSpecificExitCode	**A service-specific error code.**
CheckPoint	**An incremented value that increases as the service runs; usually zero.**
WaitHint	**An estimate, in milliseconds, of the time left before the current state completes. A value of zero indicates that there is no pending change of state.**

The last table describes status codes (as supplied in CurrentState) for a given service.

Short name	State	Description
Stopped	1	**Service is not currently running.**
Start Pending	2	**The service is scheduled to start and is currently in the wait queue.**
Stop Pending	3	**The service is scheduled to stop and is currently in the wait queue.**
Running	4	**The service is running normally.**
Continue Pending	5	**The service is currently paused but scheduled to continue shortly.**
Pause Pending	6	**The service is currently running but scheduled to pause shortly.**
Paused	7	**The service is currently paused.**

Using the information from the tables, you can find out the services on a machine by using a simple call and loop, shown here:

```
use Win32::Service;
Win32::Service::GetServices('Incontinent',\%services);
foreach (sort keys %services)
{
    print "$_\n";
}
```

Note that the server name can be any machine on the network you have suitable access rights to—you'll need administrator privileges in most situations to read and set the status of a particular service on any machine, remote or local.

The sample script on the CD is a Web-based interface to service management. Provided you have suitable access privileges, you can start and stop any service on any machine within your local network. You can see a sample of the interface—in this case accessed via a Mac—in the graphic.

Service Manager (INFURIATE)

Services for Server INFURIATE

[Clear] [Activate]

Server: INFURIATE

Service	Current	Start/Stop
Alerter	Running	Stop ☐
COM+ Event System	Running	Stop ☐
Certificate Authority	Stopped	Start ☐
ClipBook Server	Stopped	Start ☐
Computer Browser	Running	Stop ☐
Content Index	Running	Stop ☐
DHCP Client	Stopped	Start ☐
Directory Replicator	Stopped	Start ☐
EventLog	Running	Stop ☐
FTP Publishing Service	Running	Stop ☐
File Server for Macintosh	Running	Stop ☐
IIS Admin Service	Running	Stop ☐
License Logging Service	Running	Stop ☐
MSDTC	Running	Stop ☐
Messenger	Running	Stop ☐
Microsoft NNTP Service	Running	Stop ☐
Microsoft SMTP Service	Running	Stop ☐
NT LM Security Support Provider	Running	Stop ☐
Net Logon	Running	Stop ☐
Network DDE	Stopped	Start ☐
Network DDE DSDM	Stopped	Start ☐
Perl Socket Service	Stopped	Start ☐
Plug and Play	Running	Stop ☐
Print Server for Macintosh	Running	Stop ☐
Protected Storage	Running	Stop ☐
Remote Procedure Call (RPC) Locator	Stopped	Start ☐
Remote Procedure Call (RPC) Service	Running	Stop ☐
Server	Running	Stop ☐
Spooler	Running	Stop ☐
System Event Notification	Running	Stop ☐
TCP/IP NetBIOS Helper	Running	Stop ☐
Task Scheduler	Running	Stop ☐
Telephony Service	Stopped	Start ☐
UPS	Stopped	Start ☐
Windows installer	Stopped	Start ☐
Workstation	Running	Stop ☐
World Wide Web Publishing Service	Running	Stop ☐

[Clear] [Activate]

Local intranet zone

Setting up Microsoft IIS

The sample script relies on the security system under Windows NT to allow you to control the services. For the script to work, you need to set up a directory to hold the script and change the permissions for that directory to ensure that only privileged users can use it.

To set up a suitable directory, follow the steps:

1. Find your main Web server root for your machine.

2. Create a new directory; you could call it `remotemgr`.

3. Copy the script from the CD into the directory.

4. Go into the IIS manager and find the directory you have created.

5. Right-click on the directory and choose Properties.

6. Under the Directory tab, click Script under the Permissions section.

7. Within the Directory Security tab, click Edit... within the Authentication control section.

8. Make sure only the last item, Window NT Challenge/Response, is selected.

9. Click OK and then OK again.

10. For absolute protection perform steps 8 to 10 for the `svcmgr.pl` script.

From a Windows machine logged into the network, you should be able to monitor and control the machine using your normal administrator login. If you connect from another machine, you'll be prompted for an ID, password, and domain to authenticate against before the script is executed.

51 Creating Stand-Alone Windows Applications

PerlApp, part of the Perl Development Kit
ActiveState Corporation
www.activestate.com

Perl is a great language, but despite the efforts of people like you and me, it's still not a standard component of every operating system. Distribution of your scripts is therefore more difficult because they cannot be universally accepted.

The normal way of distributing Perl-based applications is to supply the Perl scripts and use a Perl interpreter installed on the local machine. There are two downsides to the practice from a developer's point of view. The first is that people could potentially steal the code you have written, to use it or to pass it off as their own. Although the possibility is not a serious consideration for some users (especially because Perl is free), it can cause problems when the scripts are being deployed in a commercial product.

The second downside to supplying scripts and using a local interpreter is that it places additional requirements onto the user when installing the software. By requiring other software to be installed—even when it's as easy as installing ActivePerl—you make the application more complex and open yourself up to all sorts of complications, which may be completely unrelated to the scripts you have distributed.

Visual Basic and C++ programmers are used to being able to distribute stand-alone applications that work and operate like other applications installed on the Windows machine. The programs don't rely on anything, except perhaps the standard Windows libraries and extensions.

I looked at some of the Perl compiler features in number 33. The C and CC backends described there can be used in conjunction with a front-end script called perlcc in order to produce a stand-alone Perl executable script. The script produces the C code, compiles it, and bonds it with the Perl libraries in order to produce the final, script-based executable.

For a variety of reasons, `perlcc` does not work under Windows at the moment. Although the modules that are used to support the back-end portion of the compiler system operate under Windows, the front-end script doesn't work properly, and it still requires a C compiler—not a standard Windows tool.

PerlApp is, however, a Windows-based solution, an additional component to the core ActivePerl distribution available as part of the commercial Perl Development Kit.

In essence PerlApp works in an identical fashion to its fairly Unix-specific cousin, but it can take a shortcut route to producing the final executable because the platform is so consistent. The same ActivePerl distribution works on Windows 95, 98, NT, and 2000 and a Windows executable works on all platforms unchanged. PerlApp thus has the flexibility to offer to different solutions to the problem.

N O T E The current version of PerlApp (v.1.2, at the time of writing) only works on Windows NT machines. However, applications built with PerlApp, even dependent ones, will work on all platforms.

PerlApp Application Types

PerlApp allows you to produce two different types of applications, a dependent and a freestanding. The dependent form essentially just embeds the Perl script into a very small application file. When executed, the application calls the Perl libraries (the Perl interpreter is located within a DLL), which in turn interprets the embedded script.

The system works very well and results in a very small application—the overhead in the format is about 7KB. The execution is also very fast—the small overhead requires little code to be loaded. DLLs are also cached, so they load almost instantaneously.

Unfortunately, for the script to execute correctly, the dependent method also requires that the end user have ActivePerl and any additional modules used by your script installed. Within a controlled environment like your machine, or those that you are in charge of, it won't be a problem; beyond the boundaries of your house, it gets more difficult.

PerlApp therefore also allows you to create a completely freestanding application. PerlApp embeds the script, the Perl interpreter (taken from its DLL), and any modules and DLLs used by your script into a single executable application. The resulting application can be executed on any machine.

On one hand, the freestanding solution implies a larger overhead; in fact, about 820K for a simple script, which potentially lowers the execution speed for short scripts. But it will make no difference with larger applications. On the other hand, it allows you to distribute applications without any worries about compatibility. In fact, MisterHouse, featured in number 43, uses exactly the freestanding system.

Converting Scripts to Applications

PerlApp uses a simple command line to turn your Perl script into its executable equivalent. PerlApp is in fact just a Perl script! In its simplest form you can turn the script `test.pl` into an application with the following line:

```
C:\> perl perlapp.pl test.pl
```

N O T E   You can use the pl2bat utility, supplied with ActivePerl, to make the PerlApp script into a more handy application. You'll find the PerlApp script in the bin directory of the base Perl installation—normally `C:\Perl`.

The PerlApp script accepts a number of arguments, as shown here in the table.

Option	Description
`-a[dd]=MODULES`	**Adds the supplied** *MODULES* **to the file created. See the section "Dependencies" for more information.**
`-c[clean]`	**Cleans up the files used during the build process.**

Option	Description
-d[ependent]	Creates a dependent application.
-e[xe]=*EXEFILE*	Creates the application with *EXEFILE*, appending the .EXE as necessary. If you don't specify the name, the script creates the application with the same name as the script.
-f[reestanding]	Creates a freestanding application.
-g[ui]	Builds an application that does not rely on a command console to operate. If you want to create such an application, you need to use Win32::Console to create your own consoles, or use Tk.
-i[nfo]=*LIST*	Adds the corresponding information to one of the property slots specified in *LIST*. This information is used to populate some elements of the Properties window in Explorer. The *LIST* should be in the form of name/value pairs separated by an equal sign, with each pair separated by semicolons. See the next table for a list of valid options.
-s[cript]=*SRC*	Uses *SRC* as the source script for the application. Uses the first script supplied on the command line if *SRC* is not specified. Note that the = character can be replaced by a space.
-v[erbose]	Generates verbose output about the production process.

The next table lists the property information for the application that you can introduce to the application when it is created.

Option	Description
comments	Comments about the file contents.
companyname	The name of the company that generated the application.

Option	Description
filedescription	A simple description of the application's purpose/abilities.
fileversion	The file version number in the form W.X.Y.Z, where each number is in the range 0-65535 and the X, Y, and Z elements are optional, defaulting to zero.
internalname	The internal name used by the application.
legalcopyright	The copyright notice for the file.
legaltrademarks	Any trademarks relevant to the application.
originalfilename	The name of the script that was used as the source of the application.
productname	The name of the overall product to which this application belongs.
productversion	The product version number in the form W.X.Y.Z, where each number is in the range 0-65535 and the X, Y, and Z elements are optional, defaulting to zero. Note that it can be a different number than fileversion.

To create a dependent application that includes the Net::FTP module, you would write the code like so:

```
C:\> perlapp -d -v -a=Net::FTP mirror.pl
Using mirror.pl for script name
Input script name: mirror.pl
Output exe name: mirror.exe
Exe Mode: Perl Dependent
Creating dependent executable
```

Dependencies

You may come across a problem when using PerlApp in those situations when a number of external DLLs are required by the Perl script. For dependent scripts you can't get around it—the Perl interpreter will include modules and DLLs if they are available on the system on which you are running the script.

For stand-alone applications you will occasionally want to forcibly include specific extensions into the final application. Normally, PerlApp will do its best to resolve and follow all the required libraries before producing the application.

The dependencies are only followed to one level to prevent PerlApp from including not only genuine DLLs but also system DLLs in the final application. If PerlApp did so, it would both be wasteful and pointless. As a good example, the Win32::Internet module, which makes use of the WININET.DLL library, produces the following output during the build:

```
Adding Module: C:/Perl/lib/Exporter.pm
Adding Module: C:/Perl/site/lib/Win32/Internet.pm
Adding Module: C:/Perl/lib/vars.pm
Adding Module: C:/Perl/lib/AutoLoader.pm
Adding Module: C:/Perl/lib/DynaLoader.pm
Adding Module: C:/Perl/lib/auto/DynaLoader/dl_expandspec.al
Adding Module: C:/Perl/lib/auto/DynaLoader/dl_findfile.al
Adding Module: C:/Perl/lib/auto/DynaLoader/
dl_find_symbol_anywhere.al
Adding Module: C:/Perl/lib/auto/DynaLoader/autosplit.ix
Adding Binary: C:/Perl/site/lib/auto/Win32/Internet/
Internet.dll
```

There's no WININET.DLL file, but no need to panic either, because that's a standard component of Windows.

In situations where you dynamically require a specific module, you'll need to use the –add option to force the inclusion of the DLL, like so:

```
C:\> perlapp -freestanding -add=Win32::Internet
```

The code will force the module (and it's dependencies and DLLs) to be added to the final executable, even though PerlApp cannot determine the dependencies at compile time.

INDEX

Note to the reader: Throughout this index **boldfaced** page numbers indicate primary discussions of a topic. *Italicized* page numbers indicate illustrations.

Symbols

.PDB (Palm Database) files, **20–22**
*roff format for Unix storage, 155
-S option for looking at subroutine trees, 126

A

Aas, Gisle, 32, 34
ActivePerl, 195, 196, 210
ActiveState version of Perl for Windows, 195
Apache
    authentication of users, **83–89**
    configuring, 88–89
        DBM and DBI configuration options (table), 86–87
        HTTPD::User Admin module, **85–88**
    CGI scripts using Perl and, **81–84**
        configuring, 82–83
        mod_perl, 83–84
    MIME file types supplied with (table), 79–80
    parsing Apache log files, **10–13**
AppleScript, communicating with, **184–186**
    about AppleScript, 184
    replying to AppleScript with MacPerl::Reply, **186**
    talking to AppleScript with MacPerl::DoApple-Script, **185**
applications
    distributing Perl-based, 208
    stand-alone, creating in Windows. *See* Windows
Archive::Tar for writing tar files directly, 173, **175**, 176
Arensburger, Andrew, 19
audio
    CDs, playing, **16–19**, *18*
        Audio::CD module, **16–19**
        CDDB (Compact Disk Database), **17–18**, *18*
        installation tips, 19
    files, reading and writing, **14–15**
        frequencies (table), 15
    MP3 for audio in homes, 180, *181*

B

Babbage, Charles, 52
backends (includes table), 128, **129–134**
    Deparse, **131–132**
    producing stand-alone scripts with, 208
    table showing list of, 129
    Terse, **130–131**
        examining compiled opcode trees, **130–131**
        examining optimizations made in compiler, **130–131**
    Xref, **132–134**
        shows detail about functions, **132–133**
        table of valid letters, 132
Barr, Graham, 99, 102, 201
BITS, 3
Brown, Martin C., 41, 72, 78, 162
Burke, Sean, 32
bytecodes, 127–128, 129

C

C::Scan module, 136
C codes, 134, 208. *See also* XtenSions (Perl)
CD-ROM that comes with this book. *See also* scripts
    CGI scripts
        for allowing users to download files without access, 81
        for converting Roman numerals, 62, *62*
        for creating and editing users in text files, 88
        for providing browsing service, 66, *67*
    data manipulation scripts
        for date, host, and page reports, 13
        script using maximal and minimal matching, 10
        scripts for error reporting, 13
        for time-logging, 4
    development tools scripts
        for building list of extensions and installing onto platform, 143
        for converting POD files to static HTML pages, 157